IF YOU'VE GOT A DREAM, I'VE GOT A PLAN

"I wish I had been able to read this book back before I learned most of what's in here the hard way. It would have saved me from some unnecessary bruises."

—BRAD PAISLEY

"Kelley Lovelace paid his dues to become a hit songwriter. By writing *If You've Got a Dream, I've Got a Plan,* Kelley has made a down payment on the dues for anyone wanting to become a hit songwriter. The information in this book will save you years in making your dreams come true."

—BRUCE BURCH, Creative Director, EMI Music Publishing, Nashville / Songwriter ("Rumor Has It" and "It's Your Call")

"I knew Kelley Lovelace when he was an aspiring songwriter hoping to get his first song recorded. He had a plan to do just that. One of my most pleasing moments since I became director of the Nashville Songwriters Association International was when "He Didn't Have to Be," hit Number 1 on the charts and Kelley stopped by NSAI to become one of our professional songwriter members. This book outlines the plan Kelley followed. It worked for him, and it can work for you."

—BARTON HERBISON, Executive Director, NSAI

"Kelley Lovelace, with his witty and very comfortable style, presents a valuable guide for songwriters everywhere who have great aspirations—yet need focus and direction to meet their dreams head-on. As a friend, I have watched Kelley follow the very plan outlined here—all the way to award-winning success. It's a plan that can work for anyone."

—SHANE BARRETT, Senior Manager, A & R, MCA, Nashville

"Songwriting not only can be fun, but it can be financially rewarding. If you're a songwriter or an aspiring songwriter who wants to learn how the music business works, then this book is a must."

—CONNIE BRADLEY, Senior Vice President, ASCAP

"I've been employed in music publishing since 1984, and I've seen "How-to-Succeed-in-the-Music-Biz" books come and go like a badly written song. However, Kelley's book is by far one of the most intelligent and insightful books I've ever read on the subject of songwriting. He is honest and fair about what is to be expected and explains how to handle yourself in publishing situations and cowrites, as well as giving advice on organizing goals and priorities. I highly recommend Kelley Lovelace's book to any aspiring songwriter."

—GLENN MIDDLEWORTH, Senior Vice President, Creative, EMI Music Publishing

"Very detailed and easily understandable, this book contains a wealth of advice and information for the aspiring songwriter."

—DON WAYNE, Hall of Fame Songwriter ("Country Bumpkin" and "Saginaw, Michigan")

"Like many of my peers, I'm often asked for advice about how to "make it" in the music business. From now on, my answer will be short and simple: go buy Kelley Lovelace's book and read it—then keep it handy because you'll want to read it again. I would be hard-pressed to think of anything about the business side of this profession that he didn't cover in a way that's easy to understand. Regardless of what level a person is on, this book is a good first step to getting to the next one up. I've always thought I know a hit when I hear one, and this is one. . . . He's done us all a service, from beginners to seasoned pros. Thanks."

—WOOD NEWTON, Songwriter ("Saving Private Malone," "Bobbie Sue," and "Twenty Years Ago")

"This fellow Kelley Lovelace is one great guy who's written one great book about making it in Nashville as a songwriter. If it'd been around in 1980, I'd have used it, day in and day out, to help me make my dream come true. If you've got the dream, get this book! Hey, and don't spend too much time thinking about Chapter 12!"

—MARK D. SANDERS, Songwriter ("I Hope You Dance," "Blue Clear Sky," and "Heads California, Tails California")

"A must read for any aspiring songwriter, written by a young man who has been there, done it, and best of all, is still in the middle of the "song wars" on Music Row. It is refreshing to see a practical, informative, and inspiring piece of work like *If You've Got a Dream, I've Got a Plan* from a songwriter who is in the thick of the music business, writing hits for the current generation."

—BUZZ CASON, Songwriter ("Everlasting Love," "Love's the Only House," and "Soldier of Love")

"Entertaining and informative. This book has great insight into this business that we call music, but is a fun read as well. It is full of realistic information that is invaluable for any aspiring songwriter who wants to "make it" in Nashville. (Plus it made me laugh out loud.)"

—FRANK ROGERS, Producer (Brad Paisley and Darryl Worley) / Songwriter ["I'm Gonna Miss Her" (The Fishin' Song), "Me Neither," and "Who Needs Pictures"]

"Kelley's years of hands-on experience as a hit songwriter in Nashville translate into a very entertaining and informative 'how-to' guide for aspiring singer/songwriters. If you're planning on coming to Nashville to pursue a career as a songwriter, I would strongly recommend you read *If You've Got a Dream, I've Got a Plan.*"

—CHRIS DUBOIS, Songwriter ("We Danced," "Me Neither," and "Wrapped Around")

If You've Got a Dream, I've Got a Plan

Foreword by
BRAD PAISLEY

KELLEY LOVELACE

THOMAS NELSON
Since 1798

NASHVILLE   DALLAS   MEXICO CITY   RIO DE JANEIRO

© 2002 by Kelley Lovelace.

All rights reserved. No portion of this book may be reproduced, stored in a retrieval system, or transmitted in any form or by any means—electronic, mechanical, photocopy, recording, or any other—except for brief quotations in printed reviews, without prior permission of the publisher.

Published in Nashville, Tennessee, by Thomas Nelson. Thomas Nelson is a registered trademark of Thomas Nelson, Inc.

Library of Congress Cataloging-in-Publication Data

Lovelace, Kelley.
    If you've got a dream, I've got a plan / foreword by Brad Paisley ;
Kelley Lovelace.
       p. cm.
    Includes index.
    ISBN 1-40160-024-7 (pbk.)
    1. Popular music—Writing and publishing. I. Title.
MT67 .L68 2002
782.421642'13—dc21   2002010245

Printed in the United States of America
02 03 04 05 06 — 5 4 3 2 1

I dedicate this book to my wife, Karen,
and to our son, McCain.
When I look at you, I see at least two reasons why I exist.

In memory of my granddaddy, Leroy Cherry.
I pray that my grandkids will love me the way I loved you.
I'll see you again someday, "Ski-daddy."

Also in memory of Randy Hardison.
I'll never walk into a studio without thinking about you.
Thanks for always taking my songs to the next level.

And in memory of Robert E. Mulloy,
the former associate dean of the
Mike Curb School of Music Business at Belmont University.
You always said, "The cream rises to the top."
I bet you've got a great view.

Contents

Foreword by Brad Paisley xi
Preface xiii
Acknowledgments xv

Introduction 1

CHAPTER 1 • **Count It Off, Boys** 3
And a 1, and a 2, and a 3, and a 4 . . .

CHAPTER 2 • **Put Me In, Coach!** 13
I know I can do it, if you'll just give me the chance!

CHAPTER 3 • **Must Be Present to Win** 27
And don't forget to bring your winning ticket.

CHAPTER 4 • **Homebound** 35
What if I don't want to or can't move to Nashville?

CHAPTER 5 • **I'm Here—Now What?** 39
Any bright ideas?

CHAPTER 6 • **Cowriting** 47
Is it remotely possible that anyone could make me better than I already am?

CHAPTER 7 • **Demos** 53
What are they, and how much do they cost?

CHAPTER 8 • **Presentation, Presentation, Presentation** 59
If you think I'm a hit song, then treat me like one!

CHAPTER 9 • **What Do I Do to Protect My Songs?** 65
Get down on your knees, bow your head, and pray!

CHAPTER 10 • **JAWS V** 71
Just when you thought it was safe to go back on Music Row . . .

CHAPTER 11 • **Nashville Needs Me!** 81
My songs are as good as, if not better than, the ones on the radio.

CHAPTER 12 • **Now That's the Life!** 89
What exactly does a full-time songwriter do all day, anyway?

CHAPTER 13 • **So What Is a Music Publisher Looking For?** 99
I can't seem to get a straight answer.

CHAPTER 14 • **Song Pluggers** 105
Are they really that important?

CHAPTER 15 • **Contracts** 109
Can't live with 'em, can't work without 'em.

CHAPTER 16 • **Show Me the Money!** 113
Advanced royalties, mechanical royalties, and what's a royalty?

CHAPTER 17 • **Show Me More of the Money!** 119
And this time, bring it to my mailbox!

CHAPTER 18 • **The Impossible** 129
What are the odds of actually making it?

About the Author 133

Index 135

FOREWORD

Brad Paisley

BREAKING INTO THE MUSIC BUSINESS AS A COUNTRY songwriter can be really difficult. Just as in any business, so many factors come into play when trying to make contacts and whittle away at your craft. It's hard enough learning to write country music effectively, with all of its structure and history. Trying to master that alone can take several lifetimes. However, let's say you are writing the kinds of songs that deserve to be recorded by superstars. Deserving this and actually getting this are two entirely different things. Okay, going further, let's say you are actually fortunate beyond all expectations and you do have the amazing opportunity to have songs published and possibly make your living as a songwriter. How do you know what kind of deal is fair? How much is your talent worth? How much can you expect to make, in a best and worst case scenario?

You're holding a book here that will address all of these questions and more. My friend Kelley not only has written a great manual for following a dream, but also has done a great service. I wish I had been able to read this book back before I learned most of what's in here the hard way. It would have saved me from some unnecessary bruises.

You know, as creative people, we writers are guilty of not always focusing on the all-important "business" of writing. And we can sometimes be extremely naive. Let this book show you where to go, what to do, and whom you need to talk to. Then you can get down to the real dream at hand: writing songs.

PREFACE

I BEGAN WRITING THIS BOOK IN 1995 SHORTLY AFTER graduating from Belmont University in Nashville, Tennessee. Actually, then it was more of a short manual for aspiring singers and songwriters. Thankfully, seven years later, Rutledge Hill Press expressed interest in publishing *If You've Got a Dream, I've Got a Plan*.

When they told me how excited they were about the book, I immediately thought, *Perfect, I've already got four hundred copies just sitting in my garage ready for distribution.* Then I thought, *This book stuff is easy. Maybe I'll whip up a mystery novel next. Yeah, something with suspense like Stephen King would write.* Slowly coming out of my dreamworld, still savoring the thought that finally someone had recognized my unique God-given gift, I heard two faint voices growing louder and louder saying, "Kelley, Kelley, Kelley!" These were the voices of Bryan Curtis and Larry Stone of Rutledge Hill Press. They politely acknowledged that though they loved what I had, they would like to suggest some changes.

Here we go. That line sounded all too familiar. I can't count the times I've heard that ego killer from a music publisher. Now I was hearing it from a book publisher too. Anyway, as is often the case, they were right.

It needed to be less of a manual and more of a book. After all, when I initially wrote it, I had just graduated from college with a degree in music business. Though I had a great deal of book knowledge, I had little if any street knowledge. You might say I was a green apple on a ripe Music Row. In fact, though I did have a music publishing deal, at that point I hadn't even had one song recorded by anyone. I guess that could have been one of the reasons I had a garage full of unsold copies.

As we were discussing various changes in content, it really started to occur to me how much more I now have to offer to other songwriters. So instead of just inserting new information into an old manual, I decided to totally rewrite it and make it a new book. So if anyone wondered where I was and what I was doing in the spring of 2002, now you know.

Acknowledgments

I KNOW THAT MOST READERS COULD DO WITHOUT THE "I couldn't have done it without you" page. However, without the support and encouragement of the following people and organizations I would never have had the opportunity to write a boring page like this attached to the front of an exciting book.

I would first like to thank Rutledge Hill Press for publishing this book. You guys have been incredible to me. I also would like to thank EMI Music Publishing for allowing me time off from writing songs to write this book. Okay, enough of the corporate schmoozing.

Mom and Dad, you know you are the single most important influence on my life. If it weren't for you, I'd probably still be in high school right now. Thanks for raising me, whipping me, grounding me, encouraging me, pushing me, teaching me, and loving me. You are the perfect example of what parents should be. I thank God for you every day.

My brothers, Grant and Cory, thank you both for not killing me while we were growing up. I love you very much.

Brad Paisley, Chris DuBois, and Frank Rogers, thank you for teaching me not to settle for average songs. You guys are the reason I have a songwriting deal today. Thanks for your wisdom and more importantly, your friendship. Oh yeah, and thanks for the great editing job on the first version of this book.

Eddie Johnson, Bill Howard, Mike Glenn, Russell Espinosa, and Bob Carter, thank you for helping me to understand God's grace and to live in the freedom and peace that Jesus Christ gives to anyone who believes in Him.

Dex, Dave, Clay, Lynn, Bearman, Ken, Zak, Ric, Johnny and everyone at US-101 in Chattanooga, I could never thank you enough for all you've done for my family and me. You guys are a big reason why my hometown is the greatest place on earth.

My friends Dave Turnbull, Tim Owens, Marc Driskill, Lee Miller, Jeff Wood, Don Sampson, Chet Biggers, and Lance Miller, my life would be less without you.

Shug Baggott, Sandy Baggott, Larry Butler, and Jerry Taylor, bless you for giving me my first job and songwriting deal in Nashville. Thanks for believing in me!

Billy and Susan Sherrill, thanks for sticking with me. I apologize for playing you all those crappy songs years ago, Billy. You started all of this!

And thank you to:

Larry Stone, Sara Henry, Jennifer Greenstein, Christy O'Flaherty, Tracey Menges, Ron Land, and the sales team. Gary Overton, Jimmy and Carolyn Gilmer, Glenn Middleworth, Bruce Burch, Bob Mather, Judy Wray, Jason Houser, Greg Hill, Emmitt Martin, Jon Sowa, Jon Mabe, Stacey Willbur, Ben Vaughn, Chris Latham, and all the EMI staff and writers. Connie Bradley, Dan Keen, Mike Sistad, Pat Rolfe, John Briggs, Ralph Murphy, Mike Doyle, Herky Williams, Chad Green, Michelle Goble-Peay, and everyone at ASCAP. Liz O'Sullivan, Steve Williams, and all the great writers at SeaGayle. Shane Barrett, Steve Weaver, Sam Ramage, Lisa Ramsey, Tim Hunze, Blake Lasater, Don King Jr. and Sr., Todd Glisson, Sheridan Lee Malloy, Mary Coleman, Rebecca Mooney, and Pat Hamilton.

Bart Herbison, Jennifer Nash, and everyone at NSAI. Jim McBride, Mark D. Sanders, Tom Douglas, Buzz Cason, Don Wayne, Wood Newton, Rick Beresfordx, C. A. Dreyer, and Joe Nichols.

LaRue Cherry (Ma), Orene Hall (Grandmother), Marie and Jack. Ronnie, Wenda, Denny, Sherry, Christa, Janeane, Garrett, Parker, and McKenzie Lovelace. Krysta and Jeff Britton. Don, Debbie, Doug,

Debbie, Bruce and Racheal Hall. Faye and Dub Smith, Jimmy, Brenda, Brittney, and Courtney Kirby. Roger, Debbie, Josh, and Adam Burrell. Shane, Tracie, Alec, and Cody Edmonson. Bobbie and Bill Marona.

Doug and Sandy Paisley. Allan Brooks and all my Station House friends. Larry and Linda Boardman, Carla, Tim, and Tracy. Karen and Curtis Settles. Jerry Whitman, Scott Morrell, Scott Shadden, Scott Vowell, Mark Davis, Scott Houghton, Glenn Czarneckie. Don, Linda, Sammy, Becky, Jay, and Laurie Benefield. Sharon, Roy, Nathan, Monica, Brent, and Heidi Ramsey. Kay and Lenard Bush. Clyde, Sue, and Brian Blaylock. Todd Zumbrun, Kim and Gary Lewis, Steve Blevins, Tommy Blevins, Todd Mayse, John Lewis, Nicky Helms, Jimmy Norris, Brian and Randy Cordell, Chuck Morgan, Freddy Johnson, Eddie, all my friends from Ryan's, and all my friends from Hixson.

Bob and Kellie Hutchins, Brad and Gene Wyatt, Michael and Tonya Moon, and all my wonderful friends in the Campbell/Young/Hannah/Steed class at Brentwood Baptist Church.

Chris Ramey, Troy Hill, Steve Kelly, Jeff Birchfeild, Patrick Fuller, Gaylen James, Steve Wright, Tony Poole, and Neil Dover.

And a special thanks to Bryan Curtis—*thank you for believing in this book.*

If your name is not in here and you feel it should be, just write it in. I'll even give it the big buildup. But most of all, I'd like to thank _____. Without you, none of this would have been possible. You're the best!

~ Introduction ~

How many times have you heard or even said to yourself, "I wish I knew *then* what I know *now*"? I don't have enough fingers and toes to count up how many times I've said that. In fact, that thought is what gave birth to this book. Well, at least part of that thought. The key difference in this cliché and the purpose of this book is that I want you to know *now* what I know *now*.

That's right! I want you to know today what it took so many other songwriters, including me, years to pick up on. Why is it that, especially in the music business, you often hear people say, "You've gotta pay your dues, man"? I'll tell you why. They want everyone else to have to suffer through learning things the way they did, the hard way. They feel that mistakes and pain are all just part of the journey. In a way, I guess it's comparable to an extremely long initiation period to a fraternity or sorority. Let me ask you: if you could bypass much of the frustration, embarrassment, intimidation, and fruitless efforts of the initiation period to the fraternity or sorority of your dreams, but still become a member, would you do it?

I haven't waited until retirement to put down my life thoughts about a craft and business that left me behind years ago. I didn't want to wait until my career was over to tell you how it was done in the good ole days. I have lived in, worked in, and studied Nashville's music business for more than ten years now, and for the last seven have made a comfortable—and lately a very comfortable—living from songwriting and music publishing. The major difference between this book and so many others out there is that as I'm writing this introduction, I can tell you about songs of mine that are currently being played on the radio, instead of reeling off titles from days gone by that you've likely never heard of.

I don't mean to slam the type of books I'm referring to—I have many of them, and they are valid and helpful. But I think it's important to mix the past knowledge of "the greats" with the present knowledge of "the goods." It's imperative to know what's going on out there right now. Has anything in Nashville's music industry changed over the years? Can education really benefit a songwriter? Let's find out!

CHAPTER 1

COUNT IT OFF, BOYS
And a 1, and a 2, and a 3, and a 4 . . .

ONE SUMMER, WHEN I WAS ABOUT ELEVEN, MY FAMILY and I loaded up to go see my aunt and uncle who live in Pine Mountain, Georgia. My uncle Ronnie, who was and still is a big-time bluegrass fan, would sit in the living room in the evenings and flat wear out the guitar and banjo. Though I liked the sound of the banjo, my beady little eyes and perked-up ears were honed in on that six-string Martin guitar. After all, to my knowledge Elvis didn't play a banjo, and if a guitar was good enough for the King then it was good enough for me too. Uncle Ron obviously picked up on my discrete drooling because before we headed back home to Chattanooga, he gave me one of his old four-string guitars and said, "If you learn how to play a song on this thing, I'll give you that Martin guitar you've been eyeballing all weekend."

I couldn't wait to get home and unleash my musical prowess on that little four-string guitar. Have you ever seen that old Robert Redford movie *The Natural*? Well, whether you have or haven't, the title itself is exactly what I wasn't. To say the least, I was anything *but* a natural. Simply holding the guitar was awkward, let alone my brain telling the fingers on my left hand to do something completely different from the fingers on my right hand. To this day I'm still amazed at how long it took me to get the pick out of the center hole of the guitar the first time I dropped it in there.

I guess you're wondering if I ever got that Martin guitar from my uncle. Truth is, by the time I got back to him to tell him I had learned a song, he had sold the guitar. *Ouch!* Yeah, I know what you must be thinking: *Bad uncle! Bad! Bad!* However, he's not the reason I didn't get that guitar; I am. Honestly, six months or more had passed before I called him to tell him that I was almost starting to get the hang of the song "Smoke on the Water." We've laughed about it many times since then. He figured that after offering me such an elaborate reward for learning how to play just one song, he would have heard from me in the first couple of weeks. After a few months went by, he assumed that I had lost interest. In part, he was right. I was continually frustrated at how difficult it was to do something that so many other people made look so easy. Though I took lessons on and off for the next few years, my dreams of dethroning the King started to diminish.

Nothing really amazing happened during my teenage years except that I survived them. Being the middle son, with older and younger brothers, I guess I felt I had to be different to stand out. Okay, I'll admit I was a bit rebellious (*sorry, Mom and Dad*). I didn't really want to go to college like my older brother had. After all, how could I be different if I did something so smart? Nonetheless, to appease my parents, I did go to college for one semester. Well, I guess it would be more accurate to say that I was on campus every day for one semester, but I actually only attended classes half the time. I did, however, become a much better pool player.

Realizing that higher education wasn't for me, I set my sights on more manly occupations. One of my first career choices was in the field of auto mechanics. I could definitely see myself working in the shop, getting all greasy fixing stuff, with a huge dip of Copenhagen in my cheek all day. You see, an occupation that wouldn't allow me to dip on the job just wasn't American to me. The only thing that kept me from pursuing this line of work was my complete lack of the necessary skills. I was one of those guys who would pull my truck out in the front yard to make sure that everyone passing by could see me changing the oil all by myself. That was really the only thing in the auto mechanic realm that I was capable of. After mentally crossing that career off, my mind began to direct me to the field of sanitation. *Yes*, I thought, *that's what I'll be: a garbage man.*

You can't find too many jobs more manly than that of a garbage man. Besides, I checked into it, and the pay was really pretty good. Again, I could picture myself hanging off the back of a garbage truck with long hair blowing in the wind and my massive biceps bulging, as I clung to the hot metal safety bar with the iron grip of one callused hand and a huge dip of Copenhagen.

Yet, as exciting and masculine as that sounded, there was something telling me that wasn't what I was meant to do. You know, if you were to take away most of the hair, the bulging biceps, the Copenhagen, the desire to be a garbage man, and then add a few pounds around the middle, you'd have a picture of me right now. By the way, your mom's right, that Copenhagen can kill you.

You'll never guess what famous celebrity was solely responsible for directing the course of my life for the next two years. It was none other than Sylvester Stallone. No, I'm not related to him in any way, and no, I didn't visit with him personally or talk with him on the phone. As a matter of fact, I have never even met him. But he did star in one of my favorite movies, *First Blood*, where he played a Special Forces Vietnam veteran named John Rambo, who happened to be traveling through the wrong town at the wrong time. He and the sheriff didn't see eye to eye, and Rambo was on the run. In one scene Sly's character has to jump off a rock cliff, though a huge pine tree amazingly breaks his fall. Rambo winds up with a nasty gash in his arm. He then grabs a needle and thread out of his survival pack and proceeds to stitch up his own arm. Now, you've got to remember at that point in my life, for whatever strange reason, I was looking for something manly, rough, and rugged to do.

After seeing that movie, that's all it took. I was Army bound! Isn't that crazy? Of course it is. It's absolutely nuts. You've also got to keep in mind that later I became a songwriter, and I can say without insult that most writers are a little different than your average Joe or, in my case, your average GI Joe.

Two important things happened to me while I was in the service. One was that I grew up a lot, and the other was that I met David "Mac" McCormick. Mac was a great friend and a phenomenal guitar player. Though he played hard rock and I was into country, I learned more about the guitar and music than ever before, and it really fired me up! I began to practice every second I could. I was eager to develop my ear for music so that I could pick off the chords of songs I heard on tapes, CDs, or the radio, and play along. The first song I learned, by listening to it over and over again, was "Your Cheatin' Heart" by Hank Williams Sr. It only took me a couple of hours to figure out all the chords. I guess I should mention that the whole song had only three chords, but like I said earlier, I wasn't a natural.

After I had played along with the tape a few hundred times, I thought it best to do something bold and move to phase two. Phase two involved playing the song without the accompaniment of the tape. You know how great you think you sound when you're singing along with the singer on the radio? Have you ever tried turning the radio completely off while you continued to sing? Most of us would probably turn the radio back on real quick before we lost the illusion that we sound just as good as, if not better than, whoever is on the radio. I think you know where I'm going here. Once I turned off the tape and began to strum the three-chord classic, I realized that maybe I *wouldn't* have been perfect to play guitar on that record. I also felt something really important was missing—and that something was the words to the song.

That's when it happened. Yep, that's when I decided that I would become a famous country music singer. As limited as I was musically, it was just too boring to sit and strum a guitar. So the decision was made, and my destiny sealed. I had no choice but to finish my time in the service and then unveil my singing talent to a world in desperate need of me and my average, yet bland, vocal style.

Realizing that I couldn't expect to take the world by storm singing other singers' songs, I began to think about writing my own. My first attempt at writing actually happened during a delayed military training exercise. Early one morning, my squad leader dropped me and our training equipment off somewhere in the middle of the woods and told me that he would be back in a little while with the rest of the squad. For the first hour or so, assuming the others would be there any minute, I just sat and enjoyed the peaceful Georgia breeze and the rare serene feeling of being alone.

After about two hours of that serene feeling, I started to get a bit restless. At nineteen years old you can crush leaves, flick twigs, and play with ants for only so long. It was becoming obvious that my faithful squad leader either had forgotten where he dropped me off or had forgotten he dropped me off altogether. I tend to think it was the latter, but that's not the point. The point is that I needed something to do to help pass the time. So I began tinkering around on my first song. I was able to finish it in a couple of hours, just in time for my squad and squad leader to arrive. He couldn't understand why I didn't act the slightest bit mad or frustrated at having been left in the middle of nowhere for half the day. The answer was folded up on a dirty scrap sheet of paper in the back pocket of my camouflage fatigues. All I was thinking about was getting back to the barracks so I could grab my guitar and put music to my first song ever. I wish I could find a copy of that old masterpiece. I'm sure you'd get a big kick out of it.

After completing my term of service, I moved back to Chattanooga, determined to join a band and begin my journey to stardom. The journey began almost immediately, but I definitely wasn't traveling in the passing lane. It kind of reminded me of when I was a kid, cramped up riding in the backseat, asking the same annoying question over and over, "Are we there yet?" It wasn't until I lucked into my third garage band that we actually played venues bigger than the garage we practiced in.

It was in one of these larger venues that a Nashville songwriter, Blake Lasater, introduced himself and asked if our band would be interested in learning and playing some of his original material. He said he wanted to see how the crowd would react to his songs. Over the next couple of weeks, I took every opportunity possible to talk with Blake and pick his brain about songwriting. When I told him about my songwriting interests and efforts, I figured he would give me the ceremonial pat on the back with a big grin and say something like, "Stick with it, kid, you'll get there someday." Incredibly, he looked genuinely excited and said, "We oughta try to get together and write one." I was blown away! Naturally, I followed up on his generous invitation, and a few weeks later we had written our first song together. Let me just say that the next thing that took place changed the course of my life forever.

Blake called me from Nashville to let me know that he had played our song for his music publisher, and his publisher loved it! He went on to say that they were going into the studio to record a more professional version of it so that they would have a better chance of getting a producer or recording artist interested in the song. He then asked if I wanted to come hang out at the studio while they recorded it. That was like asking an alcoholic if he would like to be a judge at a wine-tasting contest. Naturally, I accepted.

A few days later I found myself in the coolest place I had ever been in my whole life. I was in the control room (where all the buttons are) of a studio just outside Nashville, watching seven musicians talk about what parts they were going to play on our song. It was at that moment that I knew I wanted to be a songwriter. Not just someone who lived in Chattanooga and claimed to be a songwriter, but someone who lived in Nashville and earned a living from writing songs. Oh yes, I was hooked.

After Blake got through singing the vocal on our song, he asked if I would like to sing the song also, so I would have a version of it with my voice. Now, let me back up a bit here. Remember when I said that there was a time I thought I wanted to be and could be a famous country music singer? Well, over the past couple of years I had been singing five nights a week, at one of the bigger country bars in Chattanooga, and was slowly but surely coming to the realization that I wasn't that great a singer. On a good night I was average at best. That, mixed with the fact that I didn't really love to sing, made it easier to make the mental transition from "wanna-be" singer to "gonna-be" songwriter. I mean, I liked to sing, but I wasn't born with a desire to sing. There's a big difference. Looking back, I think my main motivation for wanting to be a singer and play in a band was to have a better chance at getting the girls. You can't blame a guy for being a guy.

Anyway, back to my taking a stab at singing our song in the studio. Part of me was saying, *Don't do it, you'll make an idiot out of yourself.* Meanwhile, another part of me was saying, *Maybe you're wrong; maybe you are a great singer.* I finally agreed and said that I would try it once just for grins. When I put the headphones on and began to sing, believe it or not, my ears were smiling at the voice they heard. Once I had finished, I couldn't wait to strut back into the control room so they could ask me if I had ever considered trying to get a record deal myself. However, beyond the casually polite "good job, man," there were no wide-eyed compliments or standing ovations.

When we listened to my song, on the big speakers in the control room, I noticed a big difference from what I had heard in the headphones. The difference was that it absolutely stunk. I mean, it Pepé Le Pew–style stunk. I asked the studio engineer why my voice sounded so much better in the headphones while I was singing. He explained that they usually put tons of vocal effects and reverb in the singers' headphone mix to build the singers' confidence by making them sound better than they really do. He further explained that if he were to put the same amount of effects in the main or final mix it would sound as if I were singing in a barrel. I wished I could have *hidden* in a barrel. With

(text continues on page 12)

Music Business 101

The music business, like other businesses, has a language of its own. Certain terms and slang terms need to be identified and explained to minimize confusion and enhance understanding. Don't worry about memorizing these terms right now. They are repeated and used in context throughout the book. By the time we reach the end, you will have a great working knowledge of them all.

Lyrics are simply the words to a song. *Melody* describes the musical accompaniment to go along with the lyrics. *Demo* is short for demonstration recording, and is a song that is captured on tape or CD that can be played back to demonstrate what has been recorded. A *guitar/vocal* or *piano/vocal* is a simple demo using only one instrument, a guitar or piano, and a singer with or without background vocals. *Background vocals* are vocals that are in addition to the lead or primary vocal. They are blended together and placed in the background to enhance the overall sound. Background vocals are sometimes referred to as *BGVs* or *harmony*.

A *music publisher* is an individual, a group of individuals, a small company, or even a large corporation whose sole reason for existence is to acquire songs to build its catalog and do everything in its power to get those songs recorded by recording artists. Once a song is recorded, the music publisher is paid royalties from the record company. These royalties, generated from record sales, are called *mechanical royalties*. If the recorded song gets played on the radio, television, or other electronic medium, the publisher then gets paid from a *performing rights organization (PRO)* for the public performances of the song. These royalties are called *performance royalties*.

A *cowriter* is a person who collaborates or works together with one or more other writers to create a song. If a writer signs one song over to a publisher, that writer signs a *single-song contract*. If a writer signs an *exclusive songwriting agreement* with a music publisher, then the writer has what is known as a *publishing deal*.

If a writer gets a song recorded by an act or recording artist, it is sometimes referred to as a *cut*. For example, a writer might say, "I got a cut yesterday or so-and-so is going to cut my song tomorrow." A cut can also be referred to as an *album cut*. A *single* is a song selected from an album or CD to be released or sent to radio to be played over the air. A single is usually a song considered to have *commercial appeal*. A song that is commercial is one that appeals to the masses or is written so that most listeners will be able to relate to it. If a song has commercial appeal and moves up the charts, it is then known as a *hit* or a *hit record*.

Song pluggers are creative people who work for music publishers. Their main function is to pitch or play songs to artists, producers, A&R representatives, and managers in hopes of getting those songs recorded. The songs they get recorded for the publisher and its writers generate royalties that are used to pay back the money the publisher has advanced (or paid up front) to the writers. An *A&R representative* works in the creative department of a record company. A&R stands for artists and repertoire, which translates to artists and songs. Hence, an A&R rep's basic function is to find artists and songs.

This is not an exhaustive list of all terms and definitions you will encounter in this book, but they are the ones that we will most commonly use. Trust that we will unpack all of this and more a little further down the road.

one last desperate attempt, I asked him if he could work some of his Nashville studio magic to make it sound at least a little better. He must have turned every knob and switched every switch two or three times, but it still didn't sound like anything I would allow anyone to hear at any time, under any circumstance.

Though that experience put the final nail in the coffin as far as singing was concerned, it in no way took away from the intoxicating excitement of songwriting. I finally knew what I was meant to do. The only thing left was to figure out the best way to go about doing it.

Thankfully, I had a great deal of help in that area. My mom and dad had always been and still are incredibly supportive of my music career. In this case, however, I've got to give the credit to my mom. She was all for my pursuing a career in songwriting, but she also wanted me to have a college degree to fall back on. She was tireless in her research efforts. I think part of her driving force came from her fear that I would revert to my old dreams of becoming an auto mechanic or garbage man. It wasn't that she thought anything was wrong with those occupations. It was that she knew my motivations for wanting to do those types of jobs were a bit whacked. I think she somehow knew I had a different calling in life, and she felt it was her job to make sure I was in the right place to hear the ring and answer it.

As the saying goes, Mom knows best. She discovered Belmont University. Unbelievably, it offered a four-year degree in music business, and better yet, was located in Nashville just off Music Row. I couldn't believe it! I immediately enrolled in a local university in Chattanooga and spent a couple of years there to get some of my general education requirements out of the way. Then I was off to Nashville to start something that still hasn't stopped.

CHAPTER 2

PUT ME IN, COACH!

I know I can do it if you'll just give me the chance!

YOU MAY BE WONDERING HOW THE HECK TO GET into the music business. There are several different ways to achieve your dreams, whether you just want to be involved somehow in the industry or want to try to make it as a professional songwriter. I firmly believe that you can do anything you set your mind to as long as your heart's in it.

I believe the best way to get rolling is to fully explore the path that worked for me. You may not have realized that there are schools set up specifically to educate aspiring music business hopefuls. I know the first time I heard that I thought my mom was trying to pull a fast one on me in her desperate attempt to get me to go to college. However, we discovered not one, but two fantastic schools close to home that cater specifically to music business students: Belmont University in Nashville and Middle

Tennessee State University (MTSU) in Murfreesboro. I attended both of these colleges and have nothing but great things to say about them.

Later I will talk about the importance of relationships and the fact that much of Nashville is composed of close-knit groups. If it weren't for one relationship in particular that began for me at Belmont back in 1993, I'm certain I wouldn't be where I am today.

When I was attending Belmont, one of the program requirements was that each music business student attend a certain number of seminars and student showcases. These showcases were organized events where students performed live to display their talent. By the way, are you the kind of person who puts everything off until the last possible minute? If so, then we definitely have more in common than our love for songwriting, because that is exactly what I did about fulfilling that program requirement. I needed one more showcase credit for the last semester of my junior year. Wouldn't you know it, it was on a Saturday night.

Saturday nights posed a special problem for me. You see, my fiancée, Karen (now my wife), lived on Sand Mountain in northeast Alabama. Naturally, every Friday after my last class I made the trek up those steep winding mountain roads as fast as I could. Captain Kirk himself couldn't have beamed me there quick enough. Yeah, I've got more than 224,000 miles on a little Toyota truck that proves my love for her.

So you see I had a dilemma. But with no other choice that weekend, I was forced to remain in Nashville and drag myself back to campus to attend the required showcase. Yes, my love would have to wait.

In a rebellious manner, I slipped into the auditorium a few minutes late and slumped into a chair in the back row. I wanted everyone to know just how disinterested I was. I wanted them to be able to see by the look on my face that this was a complete waste of my valuable time. Of course, no one really knew me, so this proved to be very ineffective.

As I sat there, bound and determined to hate everything I saw and heard, something happened that immediately began to alter my mood. A guy with a blue electric guitar began to perform with his band, and he sounded really great! I didn't know his name, but I recognized his face and guitar from a showcase the semester before. He had played lead guitar for another student, and I remembered thinking then that he was an incredible player. It didn't take me long to sit up and lean toward the edge of my seat. He had the whole place mesmerized. His voice and musicianship were smooth and unique, and his stage presence was unparalleled. Even though I enjoyed every part of the performance, what grabbed me most was his songwriting ability.

I must admit that before I heard his songs, I thought I had it all figured out. At that point, I was already writing with a few full-time songwriters on Music Row who had publishing deals with major publishers. I felt that I had my finger on the pulse of Nashville and it was just a matter of time until my career took off.

That night was extremely humbling for me. This guy sang song after song as the whole crowd hung on every word. It was then I realized that I didn't have it all figured out. I wasn't even close. My greatest songs were average at best, compared to what I heard come off that stage. At the end of the show I learned who that guy with the blue electric guitar was when the announcer said, "How 'bout another round of applause for Mr. Brad Paisley!" as Brad and his band were walking offstage.

You may think that I left there that night feeling deflated and maybe even hopeless about my career as a songwriter. Actually, I had never been so fired up to write in all my life. After hearing what I heard, I knew that good wasn't going to be good enough. The bar had been raised, and if I ever planned to jump over it, I knew I was really going to have to grow as a writer.

It hit me as I was driving back to my apartment that Brad was in my business communications class. The next morning, just before class started, he was walking by my chair and I said, "You probably already know this, but you are going to be a star." I know you've got to be thinking, "What a cheesy thing to say," right? I'll admit, I have said cooler things in my life. However, even though it did feel like a stupid thing to say, it was the only comment that fit his performance. He did a real good job of not making me feel like an idiot. He just grinned and said, "No, I don't, but thanks."

(text continues on page 18)

What If I Can't Sing or Play an Instrument?

One of the two most common questions that aspiring songwriters have asked me is, "Do I have to be a great singer to be a successful songwriter?" If the answer were yes, you wouldn't be reading this book because I never would have made it as a songwriter. The correct and direct answer to the question is *no*. You don't even have to be a decent singer to be a successful songwriter. In fact, many influential songwriters in the world either aren't able to or aren't willing to sing. On the other hand, some are more than willing to sing but probably shouldn't. No one has ever been honest with them and told them that singing is not their gift. Still other songwriters, like me, recognize that they are not really singers, but sing only to present the songs they have written.

The second most commonly asked question is, "If I don't know how to play an instrument, can I still be a successful songwriter?" Most definitely! Some successful songwriters know little if anything about music, while others know enough to confuse Beethoven. It's great if you know how to write lyrics and music, but far from mandatory.

However, if you don't play an instrument, it's imperative that you find someone who does. Because a song isn't a song without the music or melody. I'm sure that finding someone to work with will be easier for some than others, but I want to encourage those less fortunate not to give up. Think hard! Surely you know someone, or someone who knows someone, who plays a guitar or a piano. You may find this person at work, church, or right next door. Odds are that a musician of some sort lives within five miles of you. You simply have to find that person.

If you totally exhaust all your possible resources and still can't find someone musical, then you must seek other alternatives. Granted, these alternatives aren't as easy, practical, or attractive, but extreme circumstances demand extreme actions. The way I see it, you have three options. You can learn to play the guitar or piano yourself, you can move to a more populated area to increase your chances of finding a musician, or you can give up on songwriting altogether and never think of it again to avoid the torture of an unfulfilled dream. Now I know that the second and especially the third option seem a little too extreme.

Of those three options I think the first, learning how to play the guitar or piano, is the most feasible. Remember, you don't have to become an accomplished musician to be able to write songs. You just have to learn how to play well enough to create your own melodies and adequately present your songs. So don't panic. It is doable. Realize that not all hit songs are melodically complicated. Many incredible songs being recorded today have very simple chord structures and melody patterns.

If you can find someone willing to help you compose music for your song, then you've got it made. You can write the lyrics, and the other person can write the music. However, if someone other than you creates the music or melody to go along with your lyrics, that person becomes a cowriter. Your cowriter is now entitled to have his or her name on the song—it is now half your song and half your cowriter's song (more about this later). Some of you may feel that writing the lyrics is the hardest part and it is unfair to give away half of your song just for someone to put music to it. The point is that without the melody or music, all you really have is a poem. A great melody is imperative!

As brief and insignificant as that awkward encounter seemed, it marked the beginning of a friendship that has no end. The next semester we wound up having a couple of classes together and found that we had strangely similar personalities. Brad later introduced me to Chris DuBois, who at the time was a member representative with ASCAP, and Frank Rogers, a former Belmont student who worked for EMI Productions as a music producer. We all hit it off very well and, without realizing it, began to form our own close-knit group.

For those of you who don't know, Brad Paisley is an Arista Records recording artist. His current single, at the writing of this book, is "I'm Gonna Miss Her." Some like to call it "The Fishin' Song." Whatever you call it, it's a huge career record for Brad and his cowriter/producer, Frank Rogers. By the way, "I'm Gonna Miss Her" was one of the songs that Brad played at the Belmont showcase I told you about.

In addition, Brad, Chris, Frank, and EMI Music Publishing jointly own an incredibly successful music publishing company. All three of these guys, as you may already know, are extremely prolific songwriters. We all continue to write and hang out together whenever we can. Of course, it's not as easy as it used to be now that three of us are married with children. It continues to be incredibly exciting watching all our careers take off together and individually.

Back to my main point: for me, it all started at college, and this may be a good option for you, as well. At Belmont University's Mike Curb School of Music Business, you can earn a four-year bachelor of business administration (BBA) degree, with a major in music business and a minor in business administration. This is an outstanding program with phenomenal facilities. MTSU, only twenty to thirty minutes away from Nashville, offers a four-year bachelor of science (BS) degree in the recording industry, specifically designed to prepare you for a job in the music industry. The program is excellent, and the facilities spectacular.

These are both great schools, but very different. Belmont is a private school and much smaller, with an excellent student-teacher ratio; it is adjacent to Music Row, the heart of the entire music industry. Belmont is supported by many big names in the industry, such as Vince Gill, who hosts an annual celebrity basketball game on campus. Many of country's superstars show up to demonstrate how well or not so well they play the sport. MTSU, however, has a more elaborate recording facility and is much less expensive. MTSU also receives great support from the Nashville music industry.

The bottom line is that these two universities are excellent schools with unbeatable music business programs. You can get information from both and study their literature. Then set up appointments to visit each one to see what feels right.

For information on Belmont, call (800) 56-ENROLL, check out www.belmont.edu, or write to

THE MIKE CURB SCHOOL OF MUSIC BUSINESS
BELMONT UNIVERSITY
1900 BELMONT BLVD.
NASHVILLE, TN 37212-3758

For information on MTSU, call (615) 898-2578 or (615) 898-2300, check out www.mtsu.edu, or write to

MIDDLE TENNESSEE STATE UNIVERSITY (MTSU)
DEPARTMENT OF RECORDING INDUSTRY
BOX 21
MURFREESBORO, TN 37132-0001

In any event, you can't go wrong. And let me assure you that these are not the only two colleges that offer such programs. You can find them in Florida, Ohio, Boston, and California, just to name a few locations. Find a good search engine on the web and type in phrases such as "music business schools." I've stressed Belmont and MTSU specifically because I attended them both at one time or another, and because of their proximity to Music Row. Nonetheless, one of the colleges near you may offer music business programs or songwriting classes. It's worth investigating.

You can save yourself and your parents a boatload of cash by attending a small community college for the first couple of years. By doing this, you can get almost all your general education requirements out of the way at a fraction of the cost. Before registering at the community college, visit the major university you will eventually attend to make sure the courses you will be taking will transfer.

One more important point about college: *internship programs.* Just as a medical school student interns or works at a hospital for experience or school credit, a music business student can work in the music industry. Students can intern right smack dab in the middle of Nashville's music industry. This means that an intern can get on-the-job experience and training at a major record company or successful publishing company.

You may be saying to yourself, "Hey wait a minute; who said I wanted to work at a music publishing company or a record label? I want to make it as a songwriter!"

Of course you do, but before you can do anything in the music industry, you have to make contacts. Establishing contacts or relationships is exactly what you would be doing at an internship with a record company or publishing company. You may be fortunate enough to land an internship in a major record company's A&R (artists and repertoire) department or in a successful publisher's creative department. If you prove yourself an asset, odds are you'll make a fantastic contact with someone who can really help you out in the music business. Your goal should be to make friends with people like this. This is the process of networking—getting to know important people in the industry and letting others get to know you.

By interning at these prestigious and powerful companies, you will begin to establish relationships with other employees as well. This could only be positive. The more industry people you know and who know you, the better off you are and the better your chances of success. Now this is where some people will stop and say, "I knew it; it's not what you know, it's *who* you know." There's some truth to that statement, but I think it's incomplete. It's more accurate to say, "It's not what you know, it's who you know—but who you know wants to know *what* you know pretty darn quick." This expression certainly applies to the music business. The important thing to remember here is that whenever you feel you have made a contact with the right person, make sure you are ready before using that contact. You can make only one first impression, and your goal is to make it a lasting one in a very good way. A bad or ill-prepared first impression can range from very difficult to sometimes impossible to salvage.

Does everyone who obtains a music business degree achieve success as a songwriter? I'm afraid not. Though many graduates have gone on to achieve huge successes in the industry, others have found that their dream just didn't pan out. In fact, some graduates discover new dreams and change directions altogether, to work full time on the business side of the music industry. By getting exposure to various facets of the industry, some of these "star-bound" college students find that their talents might be best used as a producer, A&R representative, creative director, or even a song plugger (someone who pitches songs to record labels, producers, and artists).

These people came to town with thoughts of being a successful recording artist or a hit songwriter. However, they ended up finding interests in other areas of the business that didn't occur to them until their minds were opened up to new opportunities. They did not "fail" in any way, but merely discovered what they were really meant to do in the first place.

What if you don't want to take the school approach? College is not for everyone. Does this mean you don't stand a chance? Not a chance! That is, I mean there's not a chance that you won't stand a chance just because you don't take the university approach. Does that make sense? Okay, we're moving on.

Believe it or not, some companies will not only listen to your material but critique it as well. The Nashville Songwriters Association International (NSAI) is a tremendous nonprofit trade organization specifically designed for and by songwriters that has been helping songwriters since 1967. This organization can provide you with songwriting tips, a song evaluation service, a "ready to pitch" service, workshops, special events, counseling, a hotline, and much, much more. The membership benefits to this prestigious organization are unbeatable. I am currently and will always be a member of NSAI. If you're a songwriter and want to further your songwriting career, it's crazy not to be a member. NSAI's primary function is to protect the rights of songwriters worldwide.

The Tennessee Songwriter Association International (TSAI) is another nonprofit organization especially for songwriters. It helps writers via newsletters, information bulletins, workshops, tip sheets, critique night, Pitch-a-Pro night, Q&A, and other useful services and functions.

Another top-notch organization is the Songwriters Guild of America (SGA). For more than seventy years the SGA has provided services such as access to comprehensive legislative updates, publishing contract reviews, royalty collection, and catalog administration support. Furthermore, it offers top-quality educational workshops, seminars, and events with hit songwriters and other music industry executives.

You can also get help from the performing rights organizations (PROs): American Society of Composers, Authors, and Publishers (ASCAP); Broadcast Music, Inc. (BMI); and SESAC. These three organizations collect performance royalties for writers and publishers from radio airplay and other uses of songs, and they have representatives who correspond with writers day in and day out, in person and by phone. Some of these representatives go above and beyond the call of duty by trying to help writers find jobs or publishing deals, locate cowriters, or even make appointments with publishers.

Why would they do these things? What's in it for them? *This is important!* This "over-the-top" type of service is normally only given to those writers whom the PRO representatives feel have future earning potential. These writers, based on their present talent level, are deemed to have the potential to earn money or performance royalties with their songwriting ability at some point in the future.

The goal of all three organizations is to sign and develop as many hit songwriters as they can. The more hit songs the PROs have in their catalogs, the more leverage they have to negotiate higher licensing fees and, in turn, distribute more money to writers. The more money they have to distribute, the more appealing they will be to writers who are looking to sign for the first time or swap from their existing PRO. I don't want to get hung up too much on all this here. I just want you to be able to see the big picture.

Unfortunately, these organizations can't go "above and beyond" for every writer in the world, and I'm not saying that if you call them you will get an appointment. However, I will say they are easier to get to than you may think. For instance, ASCAP has weekly meetings open to writers and BMI has monthly meetings.

I'm sure you've heard that old saying, "Nothin' in this life is free." So I'm sure it's hard to believe that the opportunities mentioned thus far won't cost something. The truth is, some will and some won't. One of the ones that will, of course, is college. Everyone knows that an education doesn't come cheap.

The organizations I've mentioned here, however, have low or no fees. ASCAP's "Straight Talk" and BMI's "Round Table" service are *absolutely free!* NSAI and TSAI, however, charge a minimal fee for their maximum service in the form of annual dues. Currently, it costs a whopping total of $100 a year to be an NSAI member and $50 for TSAI. That averages out to about a quarter or less a day. That's couch-cushion money!

Later I will go to great lengths to warn you of "sharks" that prey on eager new songwriters, but trust me that the water is safe here. Sharks can't survive on annual dues that max out at a hundred bucks or less. Consider it an investment in your career like a guitar or any other piece of necessary equipment to get the ball rolling.

Though there may be some other worthy organizations around, I suggest you always research the company you are considering. The organizations mentioned in this book are the ones I am most familiar and comfortable with. If you have any questions about a company, a deal, or an offer that might be shady or smell fishy, call some of the organizations I've just mentioned. I bet you'll find one that will honestly answer some of your questions.

Inexpensive Assistance That Doesn't Require Financial Assistance

Nashville Songwriters Association International (NSAI). Call (615) 256-3354 or visit www.nashvillesongwriters.com. If you want to write or stop by, the address is

NSAI
1701 West End Ave., Suite 300
Nashville, TN 37203-2610

Tennessee Songwriter Association International (TSAI). TSAI meets every Wednesday from 7:00 to 9:00 P.M. at Belmont University. Locate the Jack Massey Business Center and you'll find them in Room 200B. For more information, email AskTSAI@aol.com, call (615) 969-5967, or write to

The Tennessee Songwriters Association International
P.O. Box 2664
Hendersonville, TN 37077-2664

Songwriters Guild of America (SGA). You can contact SGA's administrative executive office at (201) 867-7603; the Nashville office at (615) 329-1782; Los Angeles at (323) 462-1108; and New York at (212) 768-7902. Or visit www.songwriters.org.

American Society of Composers, Authors, and Publishers (ASCAP). You can just walk in off the street and attend one of ASCAP's 10:00 A.M. Wednesday meetings called "Straight

Talk." However, I suggest you call first to let them know you will be attending. Just call ASCAP at (615) 742-5000 or visit www.ascap.com. The address is

ASCAP
2 Music Square W
Nashville, TN 37203-3295

Broadcast Music, Inc. (BMI). BMI has meetings once a month for writers just like you. Its program, the "Writers Round Table," is designed to help inform and educate writers about BMI and what it can do for you as a performing rights organization. It also has a writer's workshop once a month hosted by hit songwriter Jason Blume (RSVP required). For a schedule, contact BMI at (615) 401-2000 or visit www.bmi.com. The address is

Broadcast Music, Inc.
10 Music Square E
Nashville, TN 37203-4399

SESAC. This organization offers a similar service to aspiring writers and will even listen to your material. However, you must be referred by a SESAC affiliate to take advantage of this. Still, you can visit their office to learn what they can do for you as a performing rights organization. Call (615) 320-0055 or visit www.sesac.com. The address is

SESAC
55 Music Square E
Nashville, TN 37203-4362

CHAPTER 3

MUST BE PRESENT TO WIN

And don't forget to bring your winning ticket.

HAVE YOU EVER SAID TO YOURSELF, "I KNOW I COULD make it if somebody important could just hear my songs"? If you really do have the desire to become a successful songwriter, then you've probably at least thought that or something similar to it.

There does come a time when hearing praise from friends and family members doesn't seem as satisfying as it once did, and you begin to crave the acceptance of the people who are really in the music business. This brings us to the not-so-popular question, "Do I have to live in Nashville to make it as a songwriter?"

Though I'm extremely inclined to say yes, let me first tell you why that simple answer doesn't suffice. Everyone has a different view of what level of success constitutes "making it" as a songwriter. For some it may be being hailed as the best songwriter in their hometown. Others may feel that they have made it by convincing their local radio station to play one of their songs on the air. Some may feel that they have achieved a certain amount of success by getting a song recorded on a small-town independent record label by an unknown artist. I think you can see what I'm getting at here. Each individual measures success differently, and there is no right or wrong way to look at it.

Though Nashville is not the only songwriting community, I do believe that if you want to establish and maintain a successful songwriting career in country music, you must live in it, around it, or at least visit it frequently. You must be present to win! Doesn't that make sense? Think about this for a moment. Let's say that two writers, both equally talented, are looking for a full-time staff writing position at a major music publisher in Nashville. One of the writers lives in Kansas and has been submitting his material to this publisher for five months trying to spark interest. The other writer has lived in Nashville for more than four years, establishing contacts by networking with other industry professionals and becoming a well-known face around Music Row. Furthermore, she has been cowriting with other writers from the same publishing company where she hopes to sign. She also has been trying to spark the interest of this particular publisher for five months by walking in the building and collaborating with its writers three days a week. Take a stab in the dark and guess which of these writers stands a better chance of landing a deal there.

Dorothy and Toto may not be in Kansas anymore, but our first writer in this example sure is. He keeps sending his songs to this publisher hoping to hear something any day. Unfortunately, his songs will probably never be heard. If anyone listens to his songs, it will more than likely be an intern, who will then send out a generic form letter that says something to the effect of, "Thank you for submitting your material. Unfortunately, it's not what we're looking for at this time. *Blah blah blah blah blah, and blah.*"

This same type of example works well when trying to explain why it's almost crazy to think that a writer who doesn't live in Nashville has a snowball's chance in the Middle East of getting a song recorded by an act on a major label. Let's use our guy in Kansas again. Let's assume that he's also been mailing his songs to record companies and producers. If by divine intervention one of his songs actually manages to levitate out of the trash can and into a listening bin full of about two hundred other songs, the miracle would still be far from complete. You see, the young woman who had been attracting the attention of the publisher by cowriting with its writers has recently had quite a bit of activity, which means she is beginning to have some success with her songs. After signing her, the publisher gets very aggressive about pitching all her songs and telling artists, record labels, producers, managers, and whoever else they're playing her songs for that she is one of the best writers to ever come to town. Again, all other things being equal, who do you think has the better shot at getting songs recorded?

Should we feel sorry for our guy out in Kansas? Would you think I was coldhearted if I said, "absolutely not"? Would you still think I was coldhearted if I added that the woman who has recently become a success is from Kansas too? The only difference between them is that she decided to actively follow her dream.

 If a guy who lives in Florida wanted to become an Olympic downhill skier, wouldn't he move to a geographic location with a climate that supports the necessary conditions? By the same token, if someone wanted to be an actress, wouldn't she need to move to Hollywood or New York to have a real shot?

Before we go any further, let me say that I know it's much easier for some to pick up and move to Nashville than it is for others. Some have made choices or find themselves in circumstances that make it extremely difficult to almost impossible to think about uprooting to pursue a dream, especially when the outcome is uncertain. I would never recommend sacrificing the happiness of a secure family to chase a dream. To many, a happy family is a dream in itself. If you are married with children and intend to move to Nashville, you will have to consider how the entire family would be affected. Personally, if I were in this position, I would have to have 110 percent support from my entire family before I took them from a place they loved to a place I'm not even sure they would like.

Now I'm not saying that every songwriter who enjoys success in the music business is, or was at one time, a resident of Nashville, nor am I saying that if you move to Nashville you'll be a huge success. I'm merely suggesting that, provided you are truly talented, living in Nashville increases your chance of success by about 95 percent. It *is* possible to get discovered in your hometown. It's also possible to get discovered or get songs cut by mailing material to Nashville. It's possible, but not probable.

You may wonder what I was referring to in the subtitle of this chapter, "And don't forget to bring your winning ticket." Well, the winning ticket I'm referring to is a hit song. Unless you are writing great songs, it is unlikely that you will get the attention you're looking for no matter how long you have lived or plan to live in or around Nashville.

So how do you write a hit song? If I knew the answer to that, I'd be living in Maui spending my days on the beach while my adoring wife fans me with palm tree branches and feeds me bite-size portions of fresh pineapple, telling me over and over again what a genius I am. All kidding aside, to my knowledge there is no set formula for writing a hit song. I can, however, offer some advice that I think will improve your writing.

Every time I sit down to write I try to remind myself of what I'm up against. About sixty other writers work at the publishing company I write for. Some write much more, but let's just say that all sixty writers complete at least one song worth pitching a week. That's a minimum of sixty new songs coming in each week. Now when the song pluggers go to their pitch meetings, trying to get the publishing company's songs recorded, they generally play only one to five songs. Let's assume the pluggers only have one pitch meeting a week where they pitch a maximum of five songs. Taking all of this into account, the result is that fifty-five other songs are turned in during a week that don't even get pitched, much less recorded by an artist.

Of course, most song pluggers have more than one pitch meeting a week, but sometimes only one or two songs are played at a meeting. And think of all the other song pluggers in Nashville vying to get their songs recorded by the same artists. In short, the competition couldn't be any tougher.

That's the mindset I begin with every day. I tell myself that unless my song is great, it won't even be pitched. This way of thinking generally steers me away from wasting time on mediocre ideas and songs. I also have found that my most successful songs—and the most meaningful to me—are the ones that are "real." They come directly from the pages of my life or from someone else's life that I'm close to. Maybe it's something that my cowriter is going through. The point is that it's easier to make a song feel real and sound real if you pull from something that really is real.

I'll be the first to admit that if you write every day you're going to run out of real material. In that case, you'll have to improvise. This is normally when I resort to pulling out my idea sheet—a list that I continually add to each time a new idea hits me. By the way, it's a good idea to have a little notepad and pencil or mini-recorder close by at all times. You never know when that great idea is going to come. It could be in the shower, during a casual conversation, while you're at work, while you're driving, or even when you're sleeping. Yes, even when you're sleeping.

I know you probably think I'm crazy, but I have honestly dreamed some really great songs and song ideas. In fact, I have won the CMA Song of the Year twice, in my dreams, with songs I have dreamed. Of course, none of those dreams came true. Do you want to know why? *Because I didn't write them down!* I would wake up in the middle of the night long enough to say, "Wow, that's an incredible song idea." Then my heavy eyes would sell my mind the same old lie, "We'll write that down first thing in the morning." Yeah, right. I've never been able to recall one yet. Ideas are funny that way. If you don't write them down, they'll fly away into the mind of someone else who will give them the attention and recognition they deserve. One thing's for sure. Ideas aren't forgiving. Once you blow them off, they never come back.

Write down every idea that pops into your head even if you think it's mediocre. What may seem to be an average idea today may surprise you tomorrow or even a few months down the road. Most of the ideas you write down won't actually turn into songs. You'll find that you'll continually cherry pick from your idea sheet.

Okay, back to writing. I think it's a good idea to try to write *visual lyrics* whenever possible. To put it another way, try to paint pictures with your words. The listener should be able to see what you have described on paper. A great example of this can be found in one of Tim McGraw's older songs entitled "One of These Days." Go back and listen to that one—I think you'll see what I want you to hear.

You also want to write as commercially as possible without compromising the integrity of the song. To write a commercial song is to write a song that will appeal to the masses or the majority of the listening or record-buying audience. Some writers feel they compromise the integrity of the song if they write commercially. They rebel against writing commercially because they feel that if they write songs trying to please everyone, they somehow will lose the uniqueness or the true character of the song. Several writers I know say things like, "I don't care if anyone gets or understands my songs; I write them for myself." Unfortunately, this type of writer is usually not monetarily successful. *Sometimes you've got to bend if you don't want to be broke.*

Coming up with unique song ideas is important. A different or interesting song idea or title can raise more eyebrows than something more generic. A&R reps from record labels, producers, artists, artist managers, and so on collectively listen to hundreds and sometimes thousands of songs each time they are looking to record a new CD.

Undoubtedly, at times songs make it to the right person but never get heard. Let's say that a well-known record producer decides to listen to one more song before making a final decision on what to record. He is already fairly satisfied with the material that has been selected, but thinks there just might be something better that he hasn't heard. But even though he is eager to find a song that may beat out what he already has, he knows that the record label and artist are growing impatient and ready to get the project underway.

So he decides to listen to just one more song. On his desk are three songs to choose from. One of the songs is entitled "I Love You More," one is called "I Still Love You," and the third is "John Deere Green." Which song do you think he chose to listen to? Which song would you choose? I think we would probably all pick "John Deere Green"—because it's the only one that is different. We can guess what the other two are about without even hearing them. But something as unique as "John Deere Green" screams, *"Listen to me, I'm different!"*

Now I'm not saying that songs without interesting titles can't be hits. After all, the title of the Tim McGraw song I suggested you listen to earlier, "One Of These Days," doesn't jump right off the page. No, there's nothing unique or eye-catching about this title at all. However, it is an incredibly written song and an undeniable smash.

Remember, there are no real set rules or formulas. I'm just trying to give you some things to think about. I don't claim to be able to tell you how to write hit songs. I don't guess it would help much either if I told you that hit songs just kind of happen. I didn't think so. However, as vague as that sounds, there's a great deal of truth to it. If you stay on the path that I think you're on, that statement will one day make more sense.

I don't want to mislead you to think that if you move to Nashville, work really hard, make contacts, hone your talent, learn the craft, and write great songs that you will be a shoe-in for a publishing deal. Ideally, you *would* land a publishing deal. However, some writers have done all of the above and have never had a publishing deal with a successful music publishing company. It may also surprise you to know that not all songwriters who have publishing deals are successful. Some have never had one song recorded by anyone.

I don't feel that everyone who has ever had the desire to write a song should consider a move to Nashville. A major decision like this should be thoroughly considered, and should not be based on the assumption that being a full-time songwriter would be fun and exciting. Though it's all of that and more, it can also be frustrating and heartbreaking. If being a songwriter is part of who you are, and you feel that you'll go crazy if you don't do everything you can to give it a real shot, then I think you should still carefully consider making the move. Everyone who moves here doesn't make it. Don't get me wrong. I'm not trying to build a fence and post big KEEP OUT signs all around Nashville. I just want to make sure you don't get your pants hung in the barbwire.

Unless you're considering taking the college route, I strongly advise you to get some constructive criticism about your writing before deciding to pick up and move. I'm not talking about friends or family members. I'm talking about music industry professionals. Tap into the resources listed in Chapter 2.

CHAPTER 4

HOMEBOUND

What if I don't want to or can't move to Nashville?

SO WHAT IF, FOR WHATEVER REASON, YOU FEEL THAT it's not possible or even necessary to move to Nashville? Can you still pursue your songwriting? You bet! This is so important. Some writers' circumstances prevent them from just picking up and moving to Nashville to pursue a wild-eyed dream. However, even if your circumstances are such that you could move on a whim, I don't recommend such recklessness.

I recommend that you do everything possible from where you are right now. NSAI, the Nashville Songwriters Association International, has ninety-plus regional workshops that give members who don't live around Nashville the opportunity for networking and furthering their knowledge of the craft and business of songwriting. NSAI also has a network of more than a hundred chapters in the United States and three foreign

More Great Resources

American Songwriter Magazine. An incredible magazine packed full of information you need to know.

AMERICAN SONGWRITER MAGAZINE
1009 17TH AVE. S
NASHVILLE, TN 37212-2201
www.americansongwriter.com • (615) 321-6096

Music Row. One of the best music industry magazines available. It's comparatively expensive, but if you can afford it, it's worth every penny. You'll know so much about what's happening on Music Row that you'll think you live right here in Nashville.

MUSIC ROW
1231 17TH AVE. S
NASHVILLE, TN 37212-2801
www.musicrow.com • (615) 321-3617

Performing Songwriter Magazine. More for songwriters who perform their own work, with many features and how-to tips.

PERFORMING SONGWRITER MAGAZINE
P.O. BOX 40931
NASHVILLE, TN 37204-0931
www.performingsongwriter.com
(800) 883-7664 or (615) 385-7796

Finally, you may want to read the book *This Business of Music* by Sidney Shemel and M. William Krasilovsky. It's not exactly a quick, easy read, but it's an incredible and invaluable reference tool.

countries. More than 125 regional workshop volunteer coordinators are trained to provide members with educational resources and guidance on the songwriting process and the business of songwriting at monthly meetings and specially scheduled events. You need to check this out.

NSAI may have something going on in your area right now! (That web address again is www.nashvillesongwriters.com.)

I also wouldn't be above hanging out at any music venue in your hometown, especially if the venue houses a live band. You never know whom you might run into. Don't be afraid to try to establish some sort of relationship with one or several of the band members. Let them know that you're a songwriter, and tell them about your aspirations. You may end up with a new cowriter or, better yet, one of the band members may put you in touch with someone who can really help you. Is this a long shot? Yes. However, remember that I met a Nashville songwriter in a bar I played at in Chattanooga, Tennessee. If I hadn't met him there, I probably wouldn't have made it here. *Leave no stone unturned.*

There is another way you can actively and effectively pursue your dreams of becoming a successful songwriter. This is a great way to slowly establish contacts, meet cowriters, and hone your craft without permanently leaving home until you find out whether or not you have what it takes. Let me share a story with you.

A good friend of mine, Tim James, is currently enjoying the sweet fruit of his hard labor. His second cut ever recently topped the Billboard charts and stayed at Number 1 for five wonderful weeks. Check this out. Tim made three or four trips a year for five years to Nashville from his home in Los Angeles. During this time, Tim managed to make some excellent contacts and develop relationships that are still strong to this day. He was able to learn what his strengths and weaknesses were, not from Mom and Dad, but from music industry professionals. This allowed his songwriting to grow exponentially, and he was eventually able to land a publishing deal that allowed him to write songs full time.

CHAPTER 5

I'M HERE — NOW WHAT?

Any bright ideas?

So he loaded up the truck and he moved from Beverly (Hills, that is). He wrote for that one publisher for a couple of years, until the company

(text continues on page 38)

closed its doors. Still without any cuts under his belt, he found himself once again without a deal. Though he did get a song recorded a few months later by a major label artist named Tim Rushlow, it wasn't enough to entice another publisher into signing him.

Not all songs that are recorded by artists on major record labels are financially rewarding. However, getting a song cut is always exciting. Part of the rush is the unknown—the sky's the limit (until you realize your song isn't getting off the ground).

For the next year Tim did what he could to stay afloat. He knew he needed to continue writing, but he also knew he needed to eat and pay the rent. He finally found a job that would satisfy those requirements. So he painted houses on Tuesdays, Thursdays, and Saturdays and wrote songs, pitched songs, and had meetings with publishers on Mondays, Wednesdays, and Fridays. Well, a year or so of paint fumes and rejections from music publishers can get to anyone. Tim had almost decided that he was going to pack it in and go back to his career in pharmaceutical sales when things really started to happen for him. The meeting that he almost canceled because his car broke down was the one that changed the course of his career and life forever. This meeting led to a couple of others, and he was eventually signed to the same publisher he still writes for today.

Just a few months into his new deal, Tim got one of his songs recorded by Toby Keith. It turned out to be the third single off Toby's *Pull My Chain* album. The song I'm referring to is "My List." You know, "under an old brass paper weight, is my list of things to do today." What a huge song! Congratulations Tim, you deserve it. By the way, I think it's your turn to buy lunch. I think you can afford it.

The thing I love about Tim's story is that he didn't just move to Nashville all of a sudden without a plan or preparation. He visited as often as he could afford and only proceeded with the move after his talent had reached a point where someone was willing to pay him for it. Sometimes it takes years to become an overnight success.

SO WHAT DO YOU DO IF YOU DECIDE TO MOVE TO Music City? The first thing you'll want to do, of course, is to return the U-Haul truck, and no matter what, always say, "It was like that when I got it." The second thing you'll want to do is to find a job.

A writing deal probably won't be the first paying gig you'll have. So unless you're fortunate enough to be able to transfer from another company, you'll most likely have to do what so many other successful writers have done: wait tables. This is by no means the only occupation available in Nashville, but the hours are great for songwriters trying to break into the business. By working nights at a restaurant, your days will be totally free to network, cowrite, schedule meetings, and attend meetings with writer organizations or publishers. I still have one of my old aprons in the back of my closet. I hope it's retired for good, but the way this business is, you never know when you might have to call it back to active duty.

The best thing you can possibly do to begin your journey as a Nashville songwriter is go to open mic nights. Held nightly in Nashville at venues all over town, open mic nights are where songwriters take turns taking the stage and performing their songs. (You may find places like this in your own hometown, so check it out.) The microphone is open to everyone. Even if you are unable or too uncomfortable to perform, I still highly recommend that you make your rounds and become a familiar face at these venues. These are some of the places where you're going to run into other writers who are doing exactly what you're doing. This can be a great way to begin developing your relationships and possibly meet a few cowriters as well.

Further, it's a good idea to be on the lookout for writer showcases. These showcases are sometimes referred to as "writers in the round" or a "writers' round." This means that three or more songwriters are at a particular venue such as The Bluebird Cafe or Douglas Corner, where they sit in a circle or line up on stage taking turns playing their songs. The great thing about this is that many times the performers you'll see and hear are hit songwriters. It's really pretty amazing. You can get lucky and just happen into a little club only to hear your favorite song being performed by the person who wrote it. If the thought of that doesn't excite the dickens out of you, then you may want to do some reevaluating. Songwriting may not be your true passion.

If you're new in town, I recommend that you fight the urge to walk up to hit songwriters at writers' nights and ask them if they will write with you. You'll save yourself from an awkward situation. Remember, it's not going to happen overnight, and successful songwriters generally write with other successful songwriters.

The best advice I can give you is to be patient. The average time to really get something going in Nashville seems to be about four to five years. I remember overhearing some big-name writers talking about that during my first internship. I thought they were crazy. At that point, I felt that I'd have this town figured out in about a year. You know what? I was wrong. I moved to town in 1992 but didn't get my first song recorded until 1997. Let me reassure you that it sure didn't feel like five years. I guess I was a struggling songwriter back then, but I don't quite remember it that way. I remember it as five of the best and most exciting years of my life.

There are many exceptions to the four-to-five-year rule. I've known quite a few writers to have success in a much shorter time, but I also know writers who have been at it for well over five years and have never really gotten anything going.

I still remember a time when I thought that if I could get only one song recorded by an act on a major label, I could die a happy man knowing that I had achieved my dream. If you're thinking the same thing, then like me, you're only kidding yourself. Because once you get a song cut, you begin to think, "You know, it would be great if it got released to radio as a single." Trying not to appear too greedy, you might follow by saying, "Even if it just reached the Top 40, I'd be satisfied." Do you really think you'll want it to stop there? *No!* You'll then start to set mental benchmarks like Top 30, 20, 15, and then the big one, Top 10. No one could ask for more than a Top 10 record, could they? "Well, why not?" you might say. "It's already so close to Top 5, what would it hurt? For that matter, it's already come so far. Wouldn't it be nice to see it go to Number 1 just to say it did?"

Yes, a Number 1 song is all you could ask for. That is, unless it gets nominated for Song of the Year or something like that. Better yet, it could possibly be in a movie. Yeah, it's perfect for a romantic comedy. What about a book? "Sure," you think, "I could write one of those little gift books that includes the CD. Then I would be more than just a songwriter. I would be an author!" So you see, it never ends.

Be honest with yourself. It's okay to want more than just one cut, and as far as I'm concerned, you're not even human if you don't care if it gets

(text continues on page 43)

Maximizing Your Open Mic Performance

Ready to play your songs for an audience other than your admiring family? Here are some ways to produce the best possible reactions to your performance.

Try to compliment the writer who performed before you when you step up or sit down to the microphone.

It's normal to be nervous. However, don't let yourself get so worked up that you don't enjoy what you're doing. The people in the audience aren't there to watch you choke and then laugh you off the stage. They are there because they love hearing new songs and new writers. The more often you perform, the more relaxed you'll become. If you hit an off note, vocally or on your instrument, don't panic. Keep on going. You won't be the only one that stumbles.

If you're going to accompany yourself with a guitar, make sure it is in tune. If it goes out of tune while you're performing, take the time to get it sounding good before singing the next song. Trust me, the audience would rather wait a few extra seconds than cringe for three minutes through the next song.

If you don't sing or perform well, you'll soon discover that you're not alone. Remember, you don't have to be a great player or singer to do open mic nights. You're performing to let others hear your songs, not your voice.

It's usually best to play songs that you are comfortable with and know extremely well. An open mic night is not the best place to try out a song you wrote earlier that afternoon. You will probably forget the words, the chords, or both.

Most crowds seem to enjoy the story behind the song. A good short setup can be effective, and it lets the crowd get to know you a little bit. But don't talk too long between songs. If you're quick-witted and have a good entertaining personality, it can add to your performance. However, if you struggle in this area, let your songs do the talking.

If you're a drinker, I'd advise you to wait until you're through playing before you empty the keg. Some writers feel that a few cold ones or a couple of pre-show shots will help loosen them up. While there may be some truth to that, there is such a thing as being too loose.

Oh, yeah, and don't announce to the crowd that you'll be signing autographs later. You may want to try a more humble approach.

released to radio a a single or not. And no matter what anyone else says, how far it goes on the charts is a big freaking deal! For some of us, it could mean the difference in whether our kids go to college or not.

Let me warn you of something. Don't expect all of your friends and family to be excited about your courageous move to Nashville. Some may even say under their breath, "I give it two months—you'll be back with your tail between your legs." Some of them thoroughly expect you to fail. Regardless of how well you eventually do for yourself, there will still be folks back home who will never acknowledge that you have achieved anything. Even Jesus said in Matthew 13:57, "A prophet is not without honor except in his hometown and in his own household." Some of the folks back home will never see you as anything special because, after all, you're just one of them.

I got a chance to witness this type of mindset last year. I was in my hometown to do a book signing at Books-A-Million for the gift book, *He Didn't Have to Be,* that I cowrote with Brad Paisley. Now keep in mind that at that point I had lived in Nashville for about nine years. I had had more than ten songs recorded by artists on major labels, and three of those were Top 5 records. About twenty minutes into the signing, an old high school buddy walked up with one of my books in his hand and said, "I been hearin' 'bout ya quite a bit on the radio." We talked about old times for a minute or two and then exchanged the usual "great to see ya." As he was walking away he turned and gave me the thumbs up, as if to encourage me, and said, "Hang in there, man, you're liable to make it one of these days."

My signature had not even dried on the book he'd bought, which I had cowritten about a Number 1 song that I also cowrote, before he had reduced my accomplishments and nine years of blood, sweat, and tears to "hang in there." I still can't help but grin every time I think about that day. There's nothing more humbling than going back home, and I go every time I get the chance.

Whether you've moved to Nashville to attend one of the universities we talked about or have simply moved on a wing and a prayer, it won't take long for you to fit right in. Nashville has got to be one of the greatest cities on the planet, and Music Row is kind of like a world of its own. It still amazes me that three or four blocks pretty much house the whole country music industry. I know it sounds a bit cheesy, but there is something magical about those three or four streets. The people are great and there's just a great buzz in the air. It's a very exciting place to be. I couldn't imagine living anywhere else, and I wouldn't be me if I were doing anything else.

Where You Can Perform in Nashville

Here are some of the great places in Nashville where you may be able to perform your songs. Instead of listing all the details here, because they could change from time to time, I'm going to steer you to a great source: Nashville Songwriters Association International, at www.nashvillesongwriters.com. You can also consult two Nashville publications, the *Nashville Scene* or *Nashville Music Guide* for current listings. (Both these have websites as well, at www.nashvillescene.com and www.nashvillemusicguide.com.) And then call the venue to double-check everything.

Antioch Bar and Grill. 2412 Antioch Pike, (615) 331-9371. Tuesday 8:00 P.M. Selected by drawing to sing with a band of session players.

The Bluebird Cafe. 4104 Hillsboro Rd., (615) 383-1461. Monday 6:00 P.M. open mic, Sunday 8:00 P.M. writers' night.

The Boardwalk Cafe. 4114 Nolensville Pike, (615) 832-5104, www.writerartist.com. Monday, Tuesday, and Thursday 7:00 P.M. writers' night, 10:30 P.M. open mic.

The Broken Spoke Cafe. Ramada Inn, Trinity Lane at I-65, (615) 262-7524. Tuesday, Wednesday, Thursday, and Friday 7:00 P.M. Late-night open mic after the scheduled shows.

Douglas Corner Cafe. 2106-A 8th Ave. S, (615) 298-1688; (615) 292-2530. Tuesday 8:00 P.M. open mic.

CHAPTER 6

COWRITING

Is it remotely possible that anyone could make me better than I already am?

Flying Saucer. 111 10th Ave. S, #310, (615) 259-7468. Show Thursday 8:00 P.M.

The French Quarter. 821 Woodland St., (615) 226-4492. Shows Sunday 6:30 P.M., Monday and Tuesday 7:00 P.M, Wednesday 7:30 P.M., Thursday 7:00 P.M. Late-night open mic after the scheduled shows.

Guido's New York Pizzeria. 416 21st Ave. S, (615) 329-4428. Scheduled evenings of original music.

Tony Wade's Hall of Fame Lounge. Quality Inn, 1407 Division St., (615) 324-0918. Sunday and Monday 6:30 P.M.; Tuesday, Wednesday, and Thursday 6:30 P.M.; Friday and Saturday 6:30 P.M. The scheduled shows feature rounds,

bands, and special guests. Late-night open mic after the shows.
12th and Porter. 114 12th Ave. N, (615) 254-7236. Monday 9:30 P.M. writers' night. Pop, rock, and alternative writers and bands; drum kit and bass amp provided. Need promo package to be considered.

And your own hometown may have similar places to perform. It may behoove you to go online to a good search engine and put in writers' night, open mic, open mic night, or other terms. You may just stumble across something in your area.

I REMEMBER A FEW YEARS BACK WHEN I SIGNED MY second exclusive songwriter's agreement. This was the first time I had been signed to write full-time. This meant that I was self-employed. That's right; technically I was my own boss. It was my show, and I could run it any old way I wanted to.

The timing couldn't have been more perfect. My wife and I had just purchased our first home. In fact, we closed on our house the same day I signed my writer's contract. That was a pretty big day. Since I was my own boss, I took the liberty of taking a few days off just to get things set up right. Just a few days, mind you, to get all the boxes unpacked, hang some shelves in the garage, and stain the porch, deck, birdfeeder, and anything else that looked like it would look better with some three-year waterproof natural wood stain. Before I knew it, those few days had turned into two whole months.

Though it would appear that I was taking advantage of a once-in-a-lifetime opportunity, that certainly was not my intent. I had convinced myself that I would spend time getting the house in order while I was thinking of great song ideas. I figured that since I was going to be writing every day it would be a good idea to stockpile several great ideas to get my first year off to a solid start. Well, my first year wasn't getting off to any kind of start at all. Sure, I came up with a few ideas, but those ideas were a long way off from being completed songs. I finally woke up and realized that I was going to procrastinate myself right out of a writing deal. I had to somehow make myself sit down and actually write because the freedom of self-employment had been deceiving me with that little voice that kept whispering, *You've got plenty of time.*

This was one of the main reasons I decided to actively seek out cowriters.

It wasn't that I didn't enjoy writing by myself. It was that I didn't trust myself to keep my nose to the grindstone. It was just too easy to write for a couple of hours and then say, "Well, that's enough for today." By having writing appointments scheduled every day, I had no choice but to head in to Music Row, sit down with another writer or two, and try to create something great.

Before that time, I had written with only a handful of people, all close friends. So to say the least, cowriting every day with someone new was quite awkward. The first few months were the worst. I discovered that although I could get along with anyone, I couldn't write with everyone. What I mean is that I was more productive with some writers than others. For me, successful cowriting requires a certain amount of chemistry. In a way, it's almost like dating.

Full-time writers do have a fair amount of pressure to produce songs that can readily be recorded. With this in mind, a smart writer must make every cowriting session count. To do this, a writer needs to separate or weed out the productive from the not-so-productive writing partners. Let me make something very clear here. If I feel that a particular cowriting situation is not working out, it doesn't mean that my cowriter is the lesser writer. In fact, if I feel that the session is not going great, my cowriter is probably feeling the same way. Nonetheless, trying to end an unfruitful writing relationship can be a bit uncomfortable. Because of this, many writers continue to book appointments with a cowriter they know they will probably never write a great song with. Breaking up is hard to do.

Now you could be asking, "Why do I need a cowriter?" That's a valid question, and for some, the answer may be, "You don't." Not all successful writers collaborate with other writers. Some writers work best alone, and they have the hits to prove it. Some writers work great alone or with other writers. Some writers, however, are at their best and get their best results when they write with someone they really click with.

After graduating from Belmont University in 1995, I was signed as a part-time writer and hired as a full-time employee for Larry Butler's publishing company, Perdido Key Music. Meanwhile Brad Paisley signed a publishing deal with EMI Music Publishing. During this time Brad and I began to write together. Both of us were a bit apprehensive at first because we knew that if it didn't work out, our friendship could suffer.

Thankfully, it couldn't have worked out better. In no more than a couple of hours we had cranked out our first song together, called "I Still Love the Night Life." Tracy Byrd cut that song on his *I'm from the Country* CD a couple of years later. After that initial, somewhat tense writing session, we were under less pressure and our songwriting seemed to get stronger as time went on. It doesn't always work when friends try to write together, but when it does, it sure is a lot of fun.

I think it is important for writers to challenge themselves by writing with people they know are better than them. Writing with Brad is a perfect example of this. I knew from his performance at Belmont that his songs blew mine away. Knowing that he was certainly capable of writing great songs without me, I knew I was going to have to bring something to the table to make it worth his while to write with me.

Since amazing him with my superior melodic skills was not an option, there was really only one thing I could do to jump-start and add to our writing session. That one thing was to bring in an idea that would be worthy of spending an afternoon on. Fortunately, he liked the idea I had, and we began an extremely successful writing relationship that led to the career I enjoy today.

Be honest with yourself and others about your strengths and weaknesses. Something that comes easy for you may be extremely difficult for someone else and vice versa. You don't have to know it all and do it all. This is the beauty of cowriting.

It wasn't always easy for me to admit to anyone, especially myself, that no matter how hard I worked, there would always be people with more natural talent. I used to think that God held his hand over certain people, like Brad, longer than others. However, the older I get, the more I'm inclined to believe that He blesses us all equally, yet differently. Our job is to figure out what we do best and embrace what and who we are, instead of questioning what and who we're not. Sometimes when two or more writers join forces, the end product comes out so much better than any one of the writers could've possibly done on his or her own, regardless of the individual's level of talent.

I'll never forget the night that Brad and I wrote a song about the relationship between my stepson and me, called "He Didn't Have to Be." Could I have written a song like that without Brad? No way! Would Brad have written a song like that without me and my relationship with my stepson? Probably not.

I want you to understand that everyone, irrespective of natural talent, has to work at being a successful songwriter. Though some have to work harder than others to acquire the same skills, the craft and business of songwriting can be learned. I have no problem telling you that I am still learning and growing as a writer. I have learned something from every cowriter I have ever written with.

When you do find a cowriter you click with, the results can be amazing. That person is usually someone who brings out the best in you, and you the best in him or her. Remember, the song is not done until you and your cowriters agree it's done. Most writers agree that no matter who contributes what during a writing session, the song's credit is still divided equally. For instance, if you and I cowrote a song together and you wrote the melody and every line of the song except for one, the song would still be split fifty-fifty. The next time we got together to write a song, it could be a totally different story. I might be the one who carried us to a finished song. This kind of extreme scenario really doesn't happen all that much. Most of the time, it's a pretty even match. However, there are going to be days when you find that you will write or contribute more than others and vice versa. Some days you're on, and some days you stink.

Let me touch on something about writing with one or more cowriters at a time. The most I've ever attempted to write with is three other writers, a total of four. Though some writers have written songs with an even bigger group, we were unable to write one line. Personally, although I have had some successful three-way writes, I find that my favorite way to go is with just one other writer. I guess the main reason is that it's much easier for two people to agree on something than it is for three or four.

CHAPTER 7

DEMOS

What are they, and how much do they cost?

Even if you have a publishing deal, here's another very important reason to consider cowriting. By collaborating with another writer who is signed to a publishing company different than yours, you're actually doubling the chances of getting the song recorded. Let me explain. Your publisher will own your half of the song, and your cowriter's publisher will own his or her half of the song. With that being the case, both publishing companies have incentive to get the song recorded. So the song pluggers at both publishing companies will be "beatin' the streets," so to speak, trying to get the song recorded. The more writers you have on a song, the greater chance you have of getting it recorded, provided all the writers write for different publishers. Of course, the more writers on a song, the less money you stand to make. A small piece of pie still tastes good, but it usually leaves you wanting another piece.

A DEMO (SHORT FOR DEMONSTRATION RECORDING) is your original material captured or recorded on a CD or audiocassette tape. Although this sounds simple, a demo can have a dramatic effect on your career, as well as make you or break you financially if you're not careful.

How much does a demo cost? The most accurate answer is that it varies. It could cost anywhere from the price of a blank cassette tape up to around $1,000 and, in some cases, even more. Let's talk about some of these variations.

First, the cost varies depending on the purpose of the demo. If the demo is just something simple that you want to keep for yourself, then it will only cost the price of a blank cassette tape. This, of course, would be a simple home recording, normally done by using a boom box or some other type of inexpensive recording device.

If the demo is meant to be submitted to a music publisher, you may want to consider taking it to the next level. Some of you may have access to a four-track or eight-track recorder. This is ideal. The quality is more than sufficient, and the price is surprisingly reasonable. If you don't have access to this type of equipment, I suggest you try to become friends with someone who does, or find a way to purchase one of your own. Normally, you can get one of these devices for anywhere between $120 and $2,400, depending on what you want. (The more expensive units are digital.) Even though I'm sure the sound is incredible on the high-end recorders, I still recommend that you stay closer to the low end.

You may be wondering, "What if I can only afford a boom-box recording? Will a successful publisher laugh at me when he or she listens to it?" Absolutely not. Most music publishers are used to hearing songs in their most primitive stage. They know that if they can hear a possible hit by listening to a low-quality recording, they have the potential to make a fortune by professionally producing it. The publisher will hire professional studio musicians to record (or demo) your song in a music studio. It's amazing what great musicians and great vocalists can do to enhance your songs.

Though I have long been a fan of four- and eight-track recorders, I've got to let you in on a little secret. Have you ever heard of a portable minidisc (MD) recorder? A handful of writers in Nashville have started using them, and I think they are the best thing since sliced bread without the crusts. The MD player/recorder is digital and no bigger than the palm of your hand. It is so much cleaner sounding than the hand-held cassette player/recorder I have been using for years. What's even better is that you can store around twenty songs on each minidisc, and even more if you are willing to sacrifice a bit of quality.

The best thing about these little babies is that you can burn the contents of the minidisc directly onto a CD. Of course, you also need to have a CD burner to take advantage of this feature. What still blows me away is that one minute I can be sitting in a room playing a guitar and singing a new song into my MD recorder and then the next I can burn the song onto a CD. It's clear as a bell. It almost sounds like it was recorded in a studio. I love it! You can pick these little jewels up for somewhere between $200 and $400. The MD model I have is a Sony MZ-G750. The CD burner I like to use is a JVC XL-R5010. These run between $400 and $500. I know all this may sound expensive right now, but once it's paid for, you can do a lot of high-quality, low-cost recording.

Now if the demo is to be pitched or submitted to an artist, a producer, or a major record label, you may need to go one step further. Now we are talking about a studio and a full-blown demo. This will run somewhere in the neighborhood of $450 to $1,500 per song. This includes studio time, studio musicians, an engineer, singers, instrument overdubs, and mixing. The difference between the high and low demo cost per song is so high because every writer has a different philosophy. Some believe that a song is not going to get noticed unless it sounds more polished, like a record, while others feel that if the song itself is strong enough, there is no need to overspend on the demo. Both points are valid, and I can't say that either one is wrong.

Personally, I guess I ride the fence on the demo budget subject. I do believe that a great song speaks for itself, but I also believe that its voice can sometimes be heard more clearly with an incredible-sounding demo. Again, there's really no right or wrong view on this one. It will always be up to each individual writer or publisher. Go with your gut!

If you do decide to "go big" and schedule a full-blown demo session, wait until you have four to five songs ready to record. You will come out much cheaper by dividing the cost among several songs than if you book the studio session for only one song at a time.

When recording a demo, writers sometimes hire singers who can imitate or sound like the artist they hope will record their song. For instance, if I'm going to demo a song that I think is perfect for George Jones, then I might hire a demo singer that can sound like him. Many writers do this so that when the artist hears the demo, he can more easily imagine himself singing it. However, this plan can backfire. If that particular artist doesn't want to record the song, then the writer will probably have to go back to the studio and record a new vocal track with a singer who has a more "middle of the road" vocal style. In other words, if George Jones doesn't record the song that was sung specifically for him, then getting that particular song recorded by another artist without changing the vocal could be very difficult.

I usually play it pretty safe by hiring solid demo singers who don't really have a certain vocal style. I do, however, try to match the song to a particular type of singer. If I have written a very traditional country song, I try to hire a singer who has at least a little bit of country flavor without overdoing it. Conversely, if I have written a more contemporary song, then I will hire a singer with a more contemporary sound. It's one of those things that you will develop a sense for as time goes on.

The cost of a demo can also vary depending on the type of song. A tender love ballad doesn't always require a full demo, for example. Sometimes a good guitar/vocal or piano/vocal is all a song like this needs. Too many instruments can sometimes be overkill and diminish the vibe or feel of a song. On the other hand, a jamming honky-tonk or contemporary up-tempo song can sometimes be fully appreciated only with a full-blown demo. It's a simple judgment call. Some songs need a great demo to have an impact, while others need very little to have that same impact.

While we're on the subject of demos, let me address something that may rub someone the wrong way. Some writers feel it's necessary to do full-blown demos of every song they write. Let me try to put this delicately. *I think that's insane!* Oops, did that slip out? It's my opinion that writers should spend money only on songs they absolutely feel are potential hits, and I don't know of anyone who sits down and writes one of those every time. Now, there may be a few superhuman songwriters out there who are rare exceptions, but I seriously doubt it. If I'm wrong, please contact me because I would love to write with you.

Many aspiring songwriters squander thousands of dollars recording their material. Someone has obviously told them, "This is the only way to compete with professional songwriters." Please don't fall for this sales pitch. This is not the only way to compete with other writers or the way to impress a music publisher. The only way to get the attention of anyone who can help you in the music business is with a great song. Without a great song, a high-priced production is absolutely worthless.

Before deciding whether to demo a song, ask yourself, "Is the song really worthy of a good demo, or is it just one of those I needed to write to get out of my system?" If the latter is true, I still recommend that you record this song—but with the simplest and most inexpensive means possible. Just sit down at home with your guitar or at your piano and sing into a boom box or any other kind of recorder. All you really need to do is adequately record your song. When you listen to what you have recorded, make sure you can understand the lyrics and hear the basic melody. If so, then you have successfully recorded your song. This type of recording is commonly referred to as a "work tape." Now type out the lyrics, wrap them around the cassette tape or CD with a rubber band, file it, and forget about it. Then go write another song. The next one could be *the* one—the one that jump-starts your career.

Now, I know that asking songwriters to be critical of their own material and honestly try to evaluate the potential of their own songs sounds futile. Truthfully, none of us likes to sit down and beat our heads against the wall for a few hours, trying to make every line great, just so that when we finish we can say, "Hmm, that didn't turn out as good as I thought it would" or "Oh, well, maybe next time." Who can do that? Generally, if I put forth the effort to write a song, then I obviously believe, at least at the time, that it has the potential of being recorded.

Seriously, we're not just doing this for fun, are we? *No!* If we were, then the title of this book would've been something like *Songwriting: A Great Way to Pass Time While Having Fun.* I'm not saying that there is anything wrong with having fun, but I don't think it's our primary goal here.

Let me offer comfort by saying that the more we mature as songwriters and professionals in the music business, the better we become at discerning between good, great, and average songs—even if they are our own. Over time, you can get to a point where you realize that everything you write is not a hit just because you like it. You'll also learn that just because you think you have written a hit song doesn't necessarily mean that you have.

Is there another way of knowing whether or not a song is worthy of a full-blown demo? Absolutely. The best thing to do is seek out several opinions. I'm not talking about moms, dads, spouses, brothers, aunts, uncles, or anyone else remotely related to you. I'm talking about music industry professionals. These are people who actually make their living by working in the music industry.

Let me share a true story with you. Sometimes people just have to learn the hard way. I've always advised writers not to spend any money on their songs unless they feel certain the songs are worth spending money on. The only problem with that advice is that many songwriters feel that every song they write is a hit. Their excitement outweighs their judgment, and they normally do something they later regret.

For example, about a year ago a young writer asked if I would give my opinion on a song he'd written. After listening to it I carefully said something to the effect of, "I think this is a nice song, but I don't think it's a

CHAPTER 8

PRESENTATION, PRESENTATION, PRESENTATION

If you think I'm a hit song, then treat me like one!

commercial radio hit." Naturally, he disagreed and kept insisting that if he did an elaborate demo of it, I would be able to hear how big a potential hit it was. Again, I tactfully reiterated the opinion that he should not spend his hard-earned money on that song. Well, $1,500 later he came back and played me the same song in a more expensive form. Did it sound better than before? Yes, it did sound a little better all polished up, but underneath it was still an average song. The point is that he didn't make the song better by spending a lot of money on it.

Consider, if you will, a rusty old bicycle. You can dig it out of the garage, dust it off, wash it up, pump some air in the tires, and put a new shiny bell on the handlebars; but when you get done, it's still going to be a rusty old bicycle.

HAVE YOU EVER ORDERED DESSERT AT ONE OF THOSE fancy restaurants where they make it look more like a piece of art than a piece of pie? Even Shoney's does a pretty good job at dressing up that hot fudge cake they serve. They bring it out with the ice cream slowly melting between two slices of cake, and hot chocolate syrup cascading down the sides. Do I even need to mention the whipped cream floating on top, just thick enough to support the weight of a bright red cherry? Do you think that dessert would still be as appealing if they just slopped it all in a bowl with no concern for its appearance? No! We would probably still eat it, but we would hope that it tastes better than it looks. The point I'm trying to make is that presentation *is* everything.

The same goes for the presentation of songs. Always take the time to make the visible part of your songs look professional. Let's first take a look at the sample lyric sheet shown in Figure 1.

By the way, the lyrics in Figure 1 are by no means an example of how to write a song. They merely show how to properly prepare and present lyric sheets.

Though some publishers and writers use punctuation when preparing lyric sheets, it's not the norm. I wouldn't concern myself with it. Remember, you're not turning the lyric sheet in to get a grade on it. Hopefully, someone is going to sing the song. If they do, no one will notice or care if the punctuation on the lyric was correct. Also, make sure the font size isn't too small. You shouldn't have to strain to see the words.

All lyric sheets will not look identical. Some songs have two verses before the chorus and some have only one. In fact, some songs begin with the chorus. Furthermore, not all songs have a bridge. (A bridge is sometimes used to break up the melody of a song to keep it from wearing on the listener before going back into the final chorus. It is more often used, however, to provide an additional lyrical twist that rounds out or provides closure to a song.) The important thing to remember about lyric sheets is to make sure that the verses, chorus, and bridge can be easily identified.

"DID I HEAR YOU RIGHT"

WRITER: Bubba Pasteur

WHY ARE YOU PACKING THAT SUITCASE
ARE YOU GOING SOMEWHERE
AND WHY ARE YOU FOLDING MY FLANNEL SHIRTS
AND MATCHING UNDERWEAR
I THOUGHT I HAD ALREADY TOLD YOU
THAT MY CAMPING TRIP'S NOT UNTIL NEXT WEEK
WHAT'S THAT, YOU SAY YOU CAN'T WAIT THAT LONG
TO BE GOOD AND RID OF ME

CHORUS
DID I HEAR YOU RIGHT
IS THIS WHAT YOU WANT
OR IS THIS YOUR IDEA
OF SOME KIND OF JOKE
IF YOU REALLY MEAN IT
I'LL LEAVE TONIGHT
I'VE JUST GOTTA KNOW
DID I HEAR YOU RIGHT

WELL YOU KNOW I THOUGHT THAT YOU WERE KIDDING
WHEN YOU SAID I WAS GETTING UNDER YOUR SKIN
AND I THOUGHT THAT YOU WERE JUST PULLING MY LEG
WHEN YOU WERE TALKING ABOUT SEEING OTHER MEN
WHEN YOU CUSSED ME OUT AND CALLED ME A LOSER
I WAS STARTING TO UNDERSTAND
BUT JUST IN CASE YOU WERE TEMPORARILY INSANE
I THOUGHT I WOULD GIVE YOU ONE MORE CHANCE

REPEAT CHORUS

BRIDGE
IT'S REALLY STARTING TO LOOK LIKE
YOU DON'T WANT TO BE MINE
BUT THINK ABOUT WHAT YOU'RE DOING
'CAUSE I'M ONLY GONNA SAY THIS ONE MORE TIME

REPEAT CHORUS
© 2002 Bubba Lamar Pasteur

Figure 1 • Sample lyric sheet

If a publisher owns the song, then the publishing company's name, along with the corresponding performing rights organization, usually is typed on the lyric sheet as well. It doesn't really matter where the writer's name and publishing company information are located. That's a personal preference.

I need to mention one more thing here. When preparing lyric sheets, there is no need to place the chord changes above the words. This is not professional. In other words, *no lead sheets!* All you need to do is type out the lyrics on a clean sheet of paper with the lyrics in CAPITAL letters. Most writers and publishers prepare lyric sheets in "all caps" mainly because they are easy to read. This is especially important if an artist is in the studio recording one of your songs. All the words need to be easily seen. Also, check over your lyrics for typos and don't forget to spell check. Keep in mind that some computer programs won't catch misspelled words if the document is in all caps. If yours is set up like this, you can either find the command that changes that function or highlight the entire lyric and change it to lowercase while you spell check. After spell checking, change it all back to uppercase.

Let's now talk about how to present the audio portion of your songs. You will need to properly label your J-cards (another name for cassette or CD case inserts) and CD labels. Figure 2 represents what these should look like when you're pitching your material.

Yours don't have to look identical, but these are good examples of ones that are professionally prepared. Here is a "generic" explanation of what should go on the J-card or CD label:

>TO: Whomever you're pitching your songs to
>FOR: The artist you're pitching your songs for
>FROM: Your name
>1) TITLE OF SONG
>2) TITLE OF SONG
>3) TITLE OF SONG
>Contact information

Figure 2 • Sample J-card for a cassette and sample CD

If you have a computer, you can take advantage of programs such as CD Label Maker. *This program and others like it are inexpensive and easy to use. It's a real time saver and it makes your CDs look extremely professional.*

When preparing your J-cards or CD labels, use a typewriter or computer if at all possible. You should also type your name, song titles, or both on the label that sticks directly on the cassette or CD. Once you have done this, fold your lyric sheet so it is exactly the size of your CD or cassette tape case. Then secure the lyric sheet on the backside of the case by wrapping a rubber band neatly around the entire case. If your CD case or jewel case is transparent, then a CD label will suffice—it's not necessary to prepare a separate J-card. By the way, CDs *are* the medium of choice nowadays.

This is as good a place as any to talk about pitching or giving your songs to artists. Don't waste your time trying to find out where all the stars live so you can throw your songs over their fence or stuff their mailbox full of them. *Rumor is they don't like that.* I guess it's kind of like littering. You might as well throw your empty Big Mac box and fries on their lawn.

I'm all for being aggressive, but there is a time and place for everything. If you're pitching without the aid of a well-known publisher or song plugger, it's highly unlikely that anyone will give your tape or CD a second glance. The only exceptions are if someone in the music industry has referred you, you have some sort of relationship or connection with the artist, your songs have been requested, or the artist recognizes your name.

CHAPTER 9

WHAT DO I DO TO PROTECT MY SONGS?

Get down on your knees, bow your head, and pray!

THOUGH THE SUBTITLE OF THIS CHAPTER IS MEANT to be humorous, it's not really a joke. I'll explain what I mean in just a minute. Protecting your songs is relatively simple: All you really need to do is to *fix your song or songs in a tangible medium of expression.* More simply, after you've recorded your song on tape or CD, and/or typed out the lyrics, you own the copyright. However, to make sure that everyone else knows that you own the copyright, you can place the information that follows on all your lyric sheets and all your cassette tape or CD labels. There are three ways to acknowledge proper copyright notification.

© 2002 John Calvin Doe
Copr. 2002 John Calvin Doe
Copyright 2002 John Calvin Doe

Take your pick. All three are correct. Notification of copyright is not absolutely necessary, but making the copyright notification visible gives some people better peace of mind.

Notification of copyright and registration of copyright are two separate things. They should not be confused! To register your copyright, you need to contact

Copyright Office
Library of Congress
101 Independence Ave. SE
Washington, DC 20559-0001

For a quicker response, call the hotline number at (202) 707-9100. When you call, request Form PA to officially register your copyright. The lines are open twenty-four hours a day, and you can leave a message on the machine. It sometimes takes a little while to get through, but they will respond. In addition, you can call (202) 707-3000 for more information about the actual registration process.

You will need to submit $30 and one copy of the best edition of your song. This copy can be on cassette, CD, record, or lead sheet, and does not have to be an elaborate demo. It can just be a simple work tape or boom box recording, as long as it's the best edition of the song. If a major label artist has recorded your song, that's the version you would send in. Once you receive the PA form, simply follow the given instructions *exactly*.

That price sounds a bit steep. You may be thinking, "Will it cost me thirty bucks for every song I send in?"

If you send in five different songs on five separate tapes or CDs, then yes, it would cost you $30 for each one. But by putting a group of songs on one tape or CD, commonly known as a compilation tape, you can reduce your cost. If you do decide to submit a compilation tape to be registered, don't forget to give the tape a name. For example, "Hit Songs of John Calvin Doe, 2002." The name you assign to the tape will be used to register your works. Just for your records, you will want to write down what songs you included on your compilation tape. If you only send in one song at a time, the title of the song itself will be used for registration.

The cost may change, of course. You can learn more and keep up with the updates by going to the website www.loc.gov/copyright.

Over the years, I've had a lot of writers ask, "Do you recommend that I register all my songs?" I have to say no. I have never found this necessary. In fact, it can sometimes be troublesome. Let's say that you *have* registered all of your songs. Finally, a music publisher decides that it likes one of your songs and wants to demo it for you, but wants some changes. Maybe the publisher doesn't like the second verse and wants you to change it to make the song more effective. Naturally, being excited that someone has finally taken notice of your songwriting ability, you say, "Sure, no problem!"

Well, really you do have a small problem. You or the publisher have to contact the Copyright Office and file an amendment. Your song has been changed, so the first registration will not cover the revised song. Not only have the lyrics changed, but ownership has changed as well. Because the publisher is fronting the money for the demo expense and will require you to sign at least a single-song contract, the publisher will now own the copyright. Hence, the copyright can't be in your name but must be in the publisher's name. All of this can be done, but it just complicates what is normally a simple procedure. Of course, this is only my opinion. You must decide what feels right for you. It's never wrong to register your songs. You just need to decide whether it is necessary.

Because registering songs can become expensive, many music publishers do not register their copyrights or songs until an artist has recorded them. Let's assume a certain publisher has a thousand songs in its catalog. At $30 per song, that could get quite expensive. Even if the songs are grouped on compilation tapes, the cost is still not necessary. Some publishers want to register only the songs that are recorded and released to the public.

This brings up an interesting question. Even if you do properly register your songs, what keeps someone else from stealing your ideas? *Nothing.* You cannot copyright or protect your ideas. You can copyright only the expression of those ideas. For example, the title of one of your songs might be "That Old Truck." Who's to say that a hundred other writers couldn't think of the exact same title all on their own? However, every song that has this title, or one similar to it, should have major differences in the story line, lyric content, and melody. It is very possible that a hundred songwriters could write a song based on the same idea, and come out with a finished product that is original and unique.

Remember the song "Rumor Has It," recorded by Reba McEntire? What about "Rumor Has It," recorded by Clay Walker? Both of these songs were big radio hits. They have the exact same title but the story line is totally different. The ideas are pretty much the same, but the expression of those ideas are unique.

I remember when I used to think that every idea I came up with was a brand-new thought that no one else on the entire planet had ever thought of before. I also remember how disheartened I was when I learned that, for the most part, that wasn't true. I was working as an intern at what was then known as Starstruck Writers Group, Reba McEntire's publishing company. Anyway, one of my prestigious, high-ranking duties was to type and file song lyrics. It was then that, with my uneducated mind, I saw something that I assumed could be nothing else than blatantly criminal. I couldn't believe it! I thought that I, a lowly intern, had uncovered one of the biggest copyright infringement cases to date right there in the middle of the office underneath everyone's nose. As I dug deeper, gathering evidence, I discovered that as many as five or six lyric files had the same song title. Oh, it gets better! I looked in each file and found that each of those songs, with matching titles, was written by a different writer. I whispered to myself, "The whole company must be in on this scandal. Oh, this is big; this is really big!"

Trying to be as discrete as possible, I nonchalantly asked my intern supervisor if she had ever noticed how many songs in the catalog had the same title yet different writers. She replied, "Oh yeah, that happens all the time." After a lengthy discussion, I came to understand that not all ideas are unique—*not even mine*. Sure, every now and then someone is bound to land on an idea that has never been thought of before. Even so, more often than not, the ideas that we all come up with have been formulated in someone else's mind as well. Again, you can't copyright or protect your ideas. You can only copyright the expression of those ideas. The best advice I can give you here is to make sure your version is better than everyone else's. That way, even if there are many similar titles, yours will be the one that stands out.

I used to worry myself to death thinking that someone was going to steal my songs. You should've seen me. Every night, in my little Nashville apartment, I would play and sing as softly as I could so that no one could hear my songs. Heck, sometimes I couldn't even hear them. But I eventually found out that I really didn't have anything to worry about. That was mainly because my songs pretty much stunk back then. They didn't stink as bad as a chicken house or a paper mill, but no one in their right mind would've tried to steal them.

Seriously though, I had heard stories about people stealing songs long before I got to Nashville, but you know what? In all the time I've lived here, I've never met anyone this has happened to. Oh sure, I've heard writers say that so-and-so stole their idea or hook. Do I believe that happens? Yes. However, I think it happens more unconsciously than not. Not too many writers out there will blatantly steal your ideas. Still, I'm very protective of my new songs and ideas. I don't go tell the world about them looking for pats on the back. I try to keep things pretty low key. That is, until one of those songs gets recorded. Then I'll go tell the world about it.

Usually, we hear of a copyright infringement case when someone from outside Nashville claims that a Nashville writer has somehow stolen all or part of a song. I'm not saying this has never happened or that it would be impossible for it to happen. Most of the time, however, the person who thinks he or she has been "robbed" is mistaken. It doesn't occur to that writer that more than one person could think of a similar or identical idea and then write a song about it. By the way, most of the time it is the writer, and not the writer's publisher, who foots the bill for legal costs.

Is there such a thing as a poor man's copyright? Yes. All you need to do is put your original song or songs on a cassette tape or CD. Place the tape or CD, along with a lyric sheet, in an envelope and seal it. Then go to the post office and send it certified mail to yourself. This means you address the envelope so that it arrives at your home. Once the envelope reaches your residence, *do not open it!* Trust me, your song is still in there. Then put the sealed envelope in a safe place, and make certain that you never open it.

Some people do this so the postage date will clearly be marked on the envelope. If they ever feel that someone has stolen their song or infringed on their copyright, they have proof that they created the song long before the other person. They would simply take the envelope that has been kept in safekeeping into the courtroom for the copyright infringement case.

So is a poor man's copyright all you need for absolute protection? Some music industry professionals think so, but there are mixed feelings on this issue. Personally, I don't believe it. I think it might be possible to persuade someone to settle out of court if you have a poor man's copyright. However, I don't think every court in the land would find this admissible. The main reason for my disbelief in this type of so-called protection is this: *If the poor man's copyright is all we need, then why is there a Copyright Office in Washington?*

CHAPTER 10

JAWS V

Just when you thought it was safe to go back on Music Row . . .

IF YOU'VE BEEN PURSUING THIS BUSINESS FOR ANY length of time, I'm sure you've heard about "the sharks." These are predators looking to devour anyone with the ignorance to come close enough to be bitten. Though they seem to be dwindling in number, they haven't officially been put on the endangered species list. So be careful. They're still out there, male and female. Their primary food source is money. They especially like the taste of cold, hard cash. However, there is a way to get rid of them: *Starve them! Stop giving them your money!*

Years ago, before I became a full-time songwriter, I ran a small music publishing company in Nashville. What never ceased to amaze me was how many aspiring songwriters, with little or no knowledge of how the music industry works, would come into my office acting as if they knew everything. I always tried to educate them as we sat there listening to and talking about their songs, but for most of them, it went in one ear and out the other.

One guy in particular would come to see me about once a month. He must have had more than two hundred songs in his catalog. Each month he would come in, play some new songs, and ask me if I was ready to sign him to a publishing deal. I would tell him that I didn't think he was ready for that, but I would continue to help him develop because I believed that he really could become a great songwriter someday. As time went on, he grew impatient and found a music publisher who gave him what he thought he always wanted—a publishing deal. He told me the name of the publisher, but it didn't sound familiar. I asked him how much money the publisher advanced him or started him out at. He said, "Money?"

I then asked how many songs he brought into the deal with him (known as a writer's Schedule A). He said, "All of them." I hesitantly asked if the contract he signed had a reversion clause to legally return the rights to his songs to him after a specified time, if the publisher hadn't gotten them recorded. He said he didn't remember anything like that. I then reluctantly asked, "Does this company have a decent track record?" In other words, have artists on major record labels recorded any of their songs?

His reply was, "I'm not sure, I never asked them."

You see he *was* able to land a publishing deal. However, he signed away the rights to more than two hundred songs that will probably never be recorded by anyone. He will never be able to get those back, and he received nothing in return for them. He wrote another thirty to forty songs for that company over the next year until his contract expired. He moved back to his hometown, and I never heard from him again.

All kinds of people from all walks of life have been taken advantage of in one way or another trying to break into the music business. They could be the smartest of the smart or the dumbest of the dumb. It has nothing to do with intelligence or the lack thereof. Though most rational thoughts are formulated in the brain, this is not the organ of concern. These sharks aim for the heart, and that is where most of us are the weakest. Some sharks want your songs, some want your money, and some just want anything they can get.

It may be necessary for you to pay for some things, but as a writer, *you should never pay a music publisher for anything.* Not even a Coke. If a publisher is interested in your songs or, better yet, interested in signing you to an exclusive deal, it will pay you or at least front the money for the cost of demos. Though most legitimate publishers will try to get as much as possible for as little as possible, they don't all expect to get something for nothing. If they want to work with you, then they must think that you or your songs have value. This is America, and things with value cost money. Fortunately, in this case, you or your songs are those things.

Be warned that not all sharks have the same eating habits. Some like to eat big and then go into hiding for a while, while others like to eat smaller portions more often. Many times these smaller ones have those little ads in the backs of magazines that say, "We'll put your poem to music" or "Send in your song, and we will demo it for you." Some even say, "Have your songs reviewed by a professional." A professional what? That person could be a professional ice skater for all we know.

Generally, the cost of these types of services is small in comparison to what we have been discussing. Instead of the big-money, small-clientele approach, this is more of a numbers game. They rack up small fees from a large customer base. A little sure can add up to a lot.

Now, can I say with certainty that all of the people who run ads aimed at songwriters are cheating people? No! In fact, I'm sure some songwriters feel that they got their money's worth, and some of the businesses believe they provide a good and fair service. That's all good and fine. My point, however, is that if your goal is to become a professional songwriter, you're probably not going to find the success you're looking for in the back of a magazine.

(text continues on page 77)

A SHARK TALE

Plenty of successful writers today can still feel the sharp pain of an old bite. I was lucky enough to talk one of my friends, Jeff Wood, into submitting his shark story. Jeff cowrote John Michael Montgomery's hit "Cowboy Love." He's also had songs recorded by Collin Raye, John Berry, Tracy Byrd, Neal McCoy, and Phil Vassar, to name a few.

Let's take a look at his story. Let her rip, Jeff.

Dreamers are easy targets for the "sharks" in Nashville. If you're not careful, you can get eaten alive, no matter how savvy a businessperson you might think you are. I learned the hard way what not to do when trying to get through the front doors on Music Row.

In May of 1993, I had just completed my second year of law school at Oklahoma City University. My mind was on the law, but my heart was in Nashville. I was playing a gig four nights a week, not only to support my way through school, but also to work on my musical chops. My real dream was to get the law degree and then move to Nashville to pursue a career as a recording artist.

After graduating from Oklahoma State University, I spent a few days with Garth Brooks, another OSU grad, in Nashville to get a feel for the music industry. Garth's first single was just out at the time, so he had a little time to show me around and introduce me to several key people on Music Row. Garth's introduction went something like this, "This is Jeff Wood. He's thinking about moving here to write songs." I thought to myself, "No, I want to be a singer and record an album." Man, was I clueless. I later learned that one of the best ways to truly get your foot in the door on Music Row is through songwriting. At the time, I realized I was nowhere near ready for the move. So I went back to Oklahoma, started law school, and started trying to write songs.

In my second year of law school, a twist of ironic events occurred that eventually got me to Nashville. One night, while I was out playing a gig, my house was broken into. Everything I owned, including my clothes, was stolen. Luckily, I had renter's insurance, and I received a check for a few thousand dollars. I then had to decide what to do with the money. I didn't really need a new TV or stereo. So I spent the money and recorded some songs I had written in a local studio. Though there was nothing wrong with doing that, looking back, I probably should have recorded only guitar/vocals. If you've got a well-written song, a good guitar/vocal will sometimes suffice for Nashville purposes, at least to get your foot in the door. That would've saved me some money. Anyway, back to the story.

Some of these "sharks" in Nashville have people working for them to scout out "dreamers" throughout the country. A lot of these so-called scouts call on local recording studios. I bet you know where this is going. One of these scouts, who represented one of the hottest producers in Nashville, sent word to my little recording studio in Oklahoma City that this producer was looking for new talent to produce. Well, you guessed it, a packet with my recording project went out the next day to Nashville, and would you believe it—there was an immediate response!

"We think Jeff Wood is a star! We would like to meet with him in Nashville on this date," etc., etc., signed, "Well-known Producer." As you can imagine, I was on top of the world. My dreams were coming true. The next week, I made the trip to Nashville to meet with "Mr. Big." When I stepped into his office, there were plaques of his accomplishments wall to wall and floor to ceiling. I truly thought I had made it. Mr. Big did everything but roll out the red carpet for me. He went on and on about how he thought I was the next Garth Brooks, and how much he wanted to produce me. He wanted to produce four songs and pitch or shop the recorded project to the record companies. He basically guaranteed me he could get me a record deal. Oh, but there was one catch—before we could move forward, Mr. Big

needed a check for $25,000. This of course, would cover all his expenses. (I later learned that the project we recorded cost roughly $3,000.)

Mr. Big assured me that I would get the $25,000 back after we got the record deal because the label that signed me would reimburse me for the costs and the recordings as part of my first album. I was able to convince my dad that this was a great investment. Believe me, my dad is one of the shrewdest businessmen I have ever known. We both looked at all the "facts" and Mr. Big's credentials and wrote the check: $25,000. Makes your stomach hurt, doesn't it? The studio time was scheduled a month later. Mr. Big wouldn't allow me to record any songs I had written. "I'll tell you what #@!? songs we will record," he yelled. Isn't it ironic that we recorded songs that he owned? I later learned that he was just producing some quality demos, at my expense, for his publishing company to pitch to well-known "already signed" acts.

When it came time to record vocals, the most important part of the recording process for someone who is shooting for a record deal, Mr. Big didn't even show up in the studio. After the recordings were complete, he wouldn't even return my calls. I later learned that Mr. Big, though at one time a very well-respected producer, was now thought of as a "shark."

Since then, I have been blessed enough to get hooked up with some legitimate people and have had several songs recorded by many major recording artists, one of which was a Number 1 song. I even had the opportunity to record my own album, on which were three Top 40 songs.

One of my goals now is to help young dreamers avoid what I went through. Please, never, never, never, ever pay anybody, no matter what their credentials, a dime to get your foot into the door on Music Row. If your songs and talent are there, God willing, it will happen!

Good luck,
Jeff Wood

Have you ever hooked up with an individual or a company that claims that it can get your songs played overseas? Apparently, these people put together a compilation CD or a CD containing many different songs, writers, or artists. They then ship it to their "contacts" abroad and somehow get or say they get the songs played on radio stations in various countries. The writers or artists are later mailed charts showing how well their songs are doing in foreign countries. I have actually had writers fax me these charts to prove to me that their song is ahead of, say, Tim McGraw's latest hit. Indeed, on the charts they sent, that is what I saw. I've even had two different songwriters gloat as they reminded me that their "overseas smash" was a song that I said was probably not strong enough to be considered by an artist on a major record label.

I said all that to say this: I still think it's a bunch of horsepucky. In the first place, I can almost guarantee you that those writers or singers had to pay somebody something to be on the compilation CD. In the second place, I don't know how reliable those charts are or where they come from. All I know is that if it's not a Billboard or R&R (Radio & Records) chart, then it doesn't mean squat to me. In the third place, no one has yet shown me a check for performance royalties on these songs. If they are somehow collecting royalties, I can't imagine that it would amount to much. I have had several Top 5 hits on the Billboard and R&R charts, and each has received considerable airplay abroad. Even so, the biggest check I have ever received in one quarter from foreign airplay was just over $2,000. Admittedly, that's better than a poke in the eye with a hot stick, but it's not exactly enough to spread out on the floor and roll around in.

 Of the more than two thousand country radio stations in the United States, only a small percentage are used to compile the country Billboard and R&R (Radio & Records) charts.

Despite my naturally sarcastic personality, I don't mean to be condescending. I'm just trying to point out that these folks probably are not coming out too good on these deals. Here again, I'm sure that some writers feel that they are getting what they paid for. Some probably feel that it's all worth it just knowing their song might be playing somewhere right now in a land far away.

I'm not trying to discourage writers from trying every possible avenue to get their talent noticed. I do believe in being aggressive. However, I think it's going to be next to impossible to attract the kind of attention you're looking for in Nashville by sending your songs thousands of miles away.

Though the sharks in this chapter are indigenous to Nashville, that is not the only place you can find them. In fact, I would venture to say that there are more sharks outside Nashville than actually in Nashville. Don't forget Jeff Wood's advice: "Never, never, never, ever pay anybody, no matter what their credentials, a dime to get your foot into the door on Music Row. If your songs and talent are there, God willing, it will happen!"

Some of you may ask, "Why would anyone pay someone to listen to their songs in the first place?" The answer is desperation. They want so badly to be heard that they are willing to do anything or pay any price. It's becoming increasingly difficult to get successful record companies and publishing companies to listen to unsolicited material. Moreover, record companies and publishing companies don't have the time or the staff to listen to every singer and songwriter in the world. They already have superstars and hit songwriters making money for them.

Record and publishing companies normally don't have to go looking for talent. Other industry professionals, with a reputation for finding great talent, normally bring the talent to them. More businesses are popping up that do "charge to listen," because it's a service that few companies provide. When there is a service being offered that few others provide, you can be certain it will have some kind of price tag. It's simple supply-and-demand economics. The supply of singers and songwriters is much greater than the demand for them. Hence, a great deal of talent goes unheard unless the writer is willing to pay for a service. As sad as it is to say, there are always people ready to take advantage of the chance to take advantage of other people.

So many people have bad impressions and misconceptions of Nashville and Music Row. Though some have actually experienced shark attacks, most have just heard either true or fabricated stories and internalized them until they believe that Nashville is a town full of crooks. *Nashville is not out to get you!* Unfortunately, we live in a world where some people choose to take advantage of the uninformed and uneducated. Thankfully, you and I no longer fall into either of those categories.

Now that you know what you know, you really have no excuse to be a victim of a shark attack. Use all of your senses, including your common sense. Keep your eyes, ears, and nose open. If it looks fishy, sounds fishy, and smells fishy—it's probably a fish. In fact, it's probably a shark.

CHAPTER 11

NASHVILLE NEEDS ME!

My songs are as good as, if not better than, the ones on the radio.

EVER WATCH ANDY GRIFFITH RERUNS? YOU KNOW, that show with Andy, Barney, Aunt Bee, Opie, Floyd, Goober, Helen, Thelma Lou, and the others in the little town of Mayberry. In one episode the deputy, Barney Fife, has an offer from another town to be its sheriff. Though he is initially excited by the offer, he winds up turning them down. In classic "Fife" fashion he grabs his belt, arches his back, sticks out his chest, takes a deep breath, grins, and says, "I can't leave Mayberry, Andy. This town needs me."

I remember feeling kind of the same way "ole Barn" did, except for me, it was about Nashville. When I lived back in Chattanooga, there were times when I would listen to the radio and say to myself, *My songs are as good as, if not better than, that.* Ever felt that way? Don't get me wrong. I didn't just sit around and bash every song I heard. There have always been some great songs on the radio, but the ones I was talking about were the real crappers. Of course, at the time, I would've given my left arm to have my name on any one of those crappers.

I'll never forget my first actual meeting with a Nashville publisher. Though it was a cowriting appointment, I was told that this guy had the power and authority to sign songwriters. Well, you know what I was thinking, right? I was thinking, *This is going to be this guy's lucky day. He probably thinks he's doing me a favor, but he'll be whistling a different tune when I play him these seven—count 'em, seven—undeniable solid gold Number 1 smash hits.* I just knew that once he heard my songs, he'd buzz the receptionist and say, "You've gotta come in here and hear this kid." After I played him the first couple of songs and he didn't buzz her in, I thought that obviously she must have gone to lunch. So I nervously continued to play and sing my heart out until I had finished all seven.

The room then became awkwardly silent as he lit up another cigarette, took a long drag, and said, "Play me that first one again."

I thought, *Now we're getting somewhere. He was probably just too overwhelmed the first time through and didn't know what to say.* I understood why he wanted to hear it again. If I were in his shoes, I would want to savor the find of a lifetime too.

Well, as usual, I was way off track. When I got through playing the first song again, he said, "Yeah, I think there's something in there we can use." I was thinking to myself, *Of course there is, it's perfect.* He then asked me if he could see my lyric sheet. After quickly glancing over it he said, "Here it is. The last line of your second verse is definitely strong enough to write a song around." I thought I was going to be sick. I had just played him seven songs that I thought would stand out as undeniable hits to anyone with half a mind, and he had the nerve to tell me that he thought one line out of seven songs had potential.

A big part of me wanted to put my guitar back in its case, head back home, and say until my dying day that that guy had no idea what he was talking about. Meanwhile, another part of me was observing all the gold and platinum records and other song achievement awards hanging from all four walls in his office. As disappointed, mad, frustrated, hurt, and skeptical as I was, the thought did occur to me that maybe he had some kind of clue.

During the four hours we spent together that day I began to slowly swallow little pieces of pride until I got to the point where I realized he was honestly trying to teach me the craft of songwriting. I learned more in that one afternoon than I could possibly have ever learned on my own.

Over the years I've learned that whether I like it or not, constructive criticism is invaluable. If we ever get to the point where we think we're above being critiqued, then we're probably missing a chance to grow and mature as a writer. If one person says something isn't quite right about a line in one of your songs, then you may want to consider taking a quick look at it. If two or three people point out the same thing, then you should probably take a long *look at it.*

Often writers believe that their ability is demonstrated somehow by the number of songs they have written. I've heard many unsigned writers make statements like, "I deserve a publishing deal—I've written more than two hundred songs." Honestly, does that sound like a good reason to give someone a publishing deal? Just because someone has written a ton of songs doesn't necessarily mean that person has mastered the craft. I have literally caught hundreds, maybe even thousands, of fish, but should I expect a bass boat company to sponsor me as a professional tournament fisherman?

The same line of thought applies to those writers who feel that they should have writing deals by now based on the amount of time they've spent doing it. I've heard comments such as, "I've been writing songs for twenty years, and I think I know what a hit is." Whether or not this person has been writing songs for twenty years can be verified. That's easy. What's more difficult to ascertain is whether or not this same writer really knows what a hit is. If we were to arrive at a definitive yes based on the fact that this person has written songs for twenty years, I would find that light minded. Just because someone does something for a really long time doesn't necessarily make that person an expert. Countless individuals have played golf all their life. This doesn't mean that they are all great golfers. Some of them, in fact, probably never learned the proper way to hold and swing the club. To this day, though they play with a passion, they make the same mistakes day in, day out, over and over again.

Do some writers need more guidance and direction than others? Certainly. Some people were just born to write songs. They are naturally inclined to it, and make it sound and look easy. On the other hand, others have the ability to be great writers but need someone with experience to help develop their skills and draw out their greatness. Still others have very little natural ability, but their love and desire for writing can sometimes outweigh their lack of ability. This type of writer is usually very good at accepting his or her limitations and humbly learning from someone who has more experience or natural talent. Is it possible for each of these three types of writers to become successful? Definitely!

One type of writer, however, is disadvantaged far more than any other. This writer will probably never get a song recorded, much less get signed to an exclusive songwriting deal by a legitimate music publisher. The type of writer I'm talking about is one who, though in dire need of it, cannot and will not take advice or direction from anyone, regardless of position, experience, or track record. He wants to one day be able to say, "I did it all by myself." I'm sure you've seen an award show or two. Have you ever heard anyone say, "I'd like to sincerely thank myself—if it wasn't for me and only me, none of this would've been possible"? Even the most incredibly talented folks in the world had some help along the way, at least at some point. Don't let pride be the thing that stands between you and an opportunity to achieve your dreams.

Let's get back for a moment to those questionable songs on the radio or songs that don't make it to the airwaves but are on the CDs you buy. Have you ever been listening to a particular song and thought to yourself, "How in the world did that one make it?" You may have even gone as far as to say something like, "If that's my competition, this is going to be easier than I thought." I don't doubt that many of you have written songs that are as good or better than the ones we're talking about. Even so, let me tell you why it's still going to be more challenging than you may think to get those songs recorded.

Nashville has long been known as a closed-door town. Though in many ways that's true, in my experience I think it can best be described as a close-knit town. If your high school was anything like mine, you may remember how all the football players and cheerleaders hung out together while everyone else talked about how much they couldn't stand them. Yet at least half of the same ones who said they couldn't stand them deep down wished they could *be* one of them.

Nashville's Music Row is much like that. It is composed of tight little groups that function very well all on their own with little to no need of outside help. It's not uncommon to hear writers on the outside of these little "cliques" say things like, "He only got that song recorded because he's a good friend of the artist." Or "I heard she gets cuts only because she's dating a record producer." Do you think there is one shred of truth to these accusations? If you said yes, I would have to agree with you. Relationships do matter!

Relationships matter in almost every field. In fact, I can't readily think of one career where "knowing someone" wouldn't help. It's just the way the world works. Remember that phrase we manipulated earlier? "It's not what you know, it's who you know, but who you know wants to know what you know pretty darn quick." Let's be realistic. I honestly don't think any artist or producer will record a song that they think is awful just because one of their buddies wrote it. You can't afford to make too many mistakes in this business. With that in mind, I believe that for the most part, artists, producers, record labels, managers, and so on do try to select and record the best songs possible. Even though I believe that to be true, let me tell you how I think a few average or weak songs make it through the song search process.

(text continues on page 87)

B SONGS

So how do weaker songs make it onto records in the first place? Here are some ways this *sometimes* happens.

- A new or unproven artist doesn't get pitched the "A list" of songs from publishers and is recording the best songs available at the time.
- Someone in the artist's camp really believes in the song. Even though most of the creative staff believes it to be substandard, it's approved based on the past success of the person who is recommending it.
- A song is part of a compromise. Maybe the record company or the producer lets the artist record a song that she believes in—on the condition that she also records a song the record company or producer believes in that the *artist* doesn't like. (This could also work in the reverse order.) Many artists have an incredible song sense while others need a bit more direction.
- An artist who isn't a really great writer demands to have one or more of his songs on all his records. To keep from rocking the boat too much, the artist is allowed to do this even if better songs are available.
- The project gets "bumped up," leaving less time to search leisurely for incredible songs. As long as there are already a few "agreed-upon hits" on the project, the producer or label may decide not to be so picky on the rest of the songs because the main purpose is to round out the project.
- The people in charge of selecting songs for the project really don't have a great song sense—they don't know the difference between a good song and a great song.

These are just some ways that weaker songs wind up on recording projects. So now when you hear that not-so-moving song on a CD, you'll have an idea how it might have ended up there.

Generally, only three to six songs per album or CD are released to radio as singles. The number of singles released off each CD is usually determined by how well it is selling. If sales continue to stay up, then the record label will probably keep promoting singles off that CD. However, if sales are down, they may decide to scrap that project altogether and go back to the drawing board. Knowing all of this, it's safe to assume that sometimes as many as four to five songs or more on a record were never even considered as potential singles.

Many times these songs aren't necessarily weaker than the songs selected as singles. Sometimes they are just not as commercial, meaning that they may not be written so that the masses or most everyone can relate to them. Other times, they are simply the weaker species. They may have been written and recorded with the intention of appealing to the masses but somehow missed the mark. These songs are easy to recognize. They are the ones you skip over or fast forward through the moment you hear the first note.

To further address the "my songs are as good as, if not better than" thought: *A hit is in the ear of the listener.* Just because I don't think a song is a hit or you don't think a song is a hit, it doesn't mean that it isn't. Several times I've heard new singles and swore that they would never make it to the Top 20. Well, what do you suppose happened? They turned out to be multiple-week Number 1 hits. Go figure.

When listening to what you may describe as a weak or average song on a CD or even on the radio, it's easy to pump yourself up and say things like, "I could write that in my sleep." Even if you think you can write circles around those songs, I think it's only fair to warn you that *those songs are not your competition.* As an aspiring songwriter, your competition is not the weakest song out there. Your competition is the *strongest* song out there. Whenever you hear an incredible song that makes you think, "Man, that song blows me away" or "That song just kills me," then you have officially heard what you are up against.

Remember when we talked about Nashville being a close-knit town? I'm going to give you the key to unlock almost every door on Music Row and enter into virtually any one of those inner circles you choose. Don't spread this around because then everybody will be trying to do it. Here goes. Are you ready? You can go anywhere you want to go if you have an indisputable, unquestionable, certifiable, undeniable hit song. This is your passport. If you have the ability to write hit songs, you won't be known as the "new guy" or "new girl" for long.

If you're a new writer trying to break into the music business and make a name for yourself, you won't be able to do it with good songs. You will have to have *great* songs! In fact, since you're a "newbie," your songs really need to be better than the best in Nashville to attract the kind of attention you're looking for.

Does Nashville need me? I have to be real honest and answer no. If I died, I think Nashville would survive. But when I pose the question a different way, the answer also comes back differently. Does Nashville need songwriters? Most definitely! Without songwriters churning out songs, Nashville would eventually collapse. Oh sure, the industry could hang on for a few years by digging into their back catalog, but eventually the gig would be up.

So I would say that makes songwriters pretty important. I think that now it may be appropriate for us, in classic "Fife" fashion, to grab our belts, arch our backs, stick out our chests, take a deep breath, grin, and say, "I gotta get to Nashville, Andy. That town needs me."

CHAPTER 12

NOW THAT'S THE LIFE!

What exactly does a full-time songwriter do all day, anyway?

The previous page is not a misprint! It is merely a visual way to answer the question, "What exactly does a full-time songwriter do all day, anyway?" There are many days that a full-time songwriter does exactly what you just did; stare at a blank sheet of paper wondering where the words are.

It is entirely possible and fairly common for one or more writers to sit in a room all day long and leave at the end of the day with nothing to show for it. You may think that a nonproductive writing day like this occurs because the writers don't know what they are doing. More often than not, however, the opposite is true. You see, sometimes experienced songwriters wrack their brains all day long trying to find a great idea to write about, rather than settling for something average just to say that they wrote a song that day.

Every day is different. One day you may be "on" and have a very creative and productive day. Driving home after a day like this you may be quietly thinking to yourself, "Man, I was great today; my publisher is not paying me anywhere near what I'm worth." The next day you may have a terrible day and be thinking as you're driving home, "Who am I kidding, I'm not good enough to do this for a living. My publisher is paying me way too much money. I'm living a lie. If they only knew . . ."

Okay, let's get down to talking about a day in the life of a full-time songwriter. All songwriters differ in many areas, especially in the area of work ethic. Some writers have an incredible work ethic, writing every day from, say, 10:00 A.M. to 5:00 P.M. or even later. Some write day and night while others only write two or three times a week.

A writer's publisher doesn't care how much or when he or she chooses to write as long as the writer delivers hit songs. That is, of course, as long as the writer is fulfilling the minimum commitment of songs specified—that is, the number of whole compositions or songs the writer is obligated to deliver to the publisher each quarter, half year, or year depending on the contract. Did you notice the word *whole* in that last sentence? That means whole songs. For example, let's say a writer's minimum commitment or minimum song delivery is ten songs per year. If the writer writes ten songs alone, then the commitment would be fulfilled. However, if this writer always writes with a cowriter, then the number of songs needed to fulfill the commitment would double to twenty because he or she is only writing "half" a song. If the song has three writers, our writer gets "one-third" credit, and must turn in thirty of these cowritten songs to meet the minimum commitment. In short, the more writers on each song, the more songs the writer must write to fulfill that commitment.

Some writers don't take their minimum commitment (also known as a quota) very seriously, especially if they are earning a lot of money for their publisher. However, in order to abide by the terms of their contract, they will sometimes just barely slip in the right amount of songs. These last minute "quota songs" can be quite hilarious. They can range from simple one-chord instrumentals to actual songs that lyrically sound like nothing but random thoughts. The best one I've ever heard is one a couple of my buddies wrote called "The Quota Song." It has lines in it like, "Oh, I'm writing this song to fill my quota. . . ."

Anyway, most staff writers arrive at their publishing company or their cowriter's publishing company at the crack of 10:00 A.M. I know it sounds awful early, but if you want to get anywhere in life, you've got to get an early start. The first order of business is to gather around the coffeepot, fix a cup, and shoot the bull until you get good and awake. That usually takes until about 10:30 A.M. By then everyone is feeling the pressure to break it up, head to a writer's room, and get started. A writer's room is just what you think—a room at a publishing company designated for songwriters to write in. Some writer's rooms have nice furniture, windows, paintings or pictures, colorful walls, and recording equipment, while others basically have two chairs and a table.

Although most Nashville writers carry their guitars to Music Row every day, some lug around small keyboards. Some don't even carry an instrument at all. Lyricists, who write only words for songs, may use a laptop computer or simply a pencil and a writing pad.

Once in the writer's room, the writer or writers sort through ideas and presumably land on one worthy of committing to. By the time a good idea is found or agreed upon, it's usually time for lunch. I love lunch! After topping off, it's time to crack that whip again and get back to work. The end of the day could come at 2:00, 3:00, 5:00, 6:00 or even 10:00 P.M. Though in some cases it could spill over into the A.M. hours, most songwriters with families call it quits no later than late afternoon. Remember, each individual is different. There are no set times except the times the writers set for themselves. Most full-time writers are in charge of their own schedule.

It would certainly seem that, with this type of schedule, songwriters really have it made. In many ways, they do. Personally, I can't think of a more perfect occupation. However, this incredible career has not just one but several downsides.

Over the years I've gotten to know some pretty interesting people in all facets of the entertainment industry. If I've learned one thing through these relationships, it's that a certain amount of crap goes along with every kind of job in the world. I like to refer to it as "the crap factor." Though some jobs have a higher crap factor than others, they all have some degree of it, without exception.

Wouldn't it be incredible if all that songwriters had to do every day was just write life-changing songs? Even if that were true, it would be virtually impossible. I don't know anyone who can crank out incredible songs at will. But even if they could, this occupation still wouldn't be without flaws.

One thing that can fall into the crap factor category is playing new songs for song pluggers, which can sometimes be a very unpleasant experience. When a writer feels he or she has written a great song and gets only a mild to lukewarm response from the plugger, this can be a real letdown to say the least. Regardless of how the writer feels about a song, it's impossible to make someone like something.

Not all writers, but most, must have their pluggers approve their songs before they can take them to the next level. That next level would be selecting four or five new songs and scheduling a demo session to produce professional full-blown demos to be pitched to recording artists. If a plugger doesn't believe in a song that the writer believes in, that song may not be approved for the demo session. This can be frustrating. However, most writers realize there's not much point in doing a demo of a song a plugger doesn't like. Point being, if the plugger doesn't like it, the plugger probably won't pitch it. Some veteran songwriters with several hits under their belt may not worry as much as younger writers about what their plugger doesn't like. Because of their name and track record, the veteran writers may be successful pitching their songs themselves.

While we're on the subject of demo sessions, I might as well mention that this process can sometimes be a headache for a full-time songwriter. Though some music publishers help their writers schedule sessions, many do not. This means that the writer is responsible for booking studio time, engineers, musicians, and singers. This can get complicated and even a little stressful. It's next to impossible to find and schedule a particular day where you can get the studio you want, the engineer you want, the musicians you want, and the singers you want. There always seems to be some sort of conflict. You can imagine how difficult scheduling could be. More often than not, you have to compromise somewhere.

Once everything is scheduled, there is one other small area of concern. Will everyone you booked show up? You never know when people you have scheduled weeks in advance will call at the last minute with a good or bad excuse for why they can't be there.

Assuming that, by the grace of God, the session goes smoothly, the writer is in for a month that can be both exciting and disappointing. Generally, once the session is turned in to the publishing company, the pluggers immediately hit the streets. If they really believe in the songs they are pitching, they will do everything in their power to place those songs with an act on a major label.

During this time, the writers are anxiously anticipating a call. Sometimes they will get one to say that an artist, record company, producer, or manager has placed a song "on hold." Having a hold is a good thing. It means that the person who likes the song is requesting that the plugger hold onto or not pitch that song to anyone else until he gets back with the plugger to say whether he plans to record it or pass on it.

As you can see, a hold in no way guarantees that the song will be cut. Most songs on hold *don't* get recorded. Keep in mind that if a record company or producer has forty songs or more on hold for an artist, that means when they select ten to fourteen songs to record, more than half of the songs that were on hold become songs that have been passed on. Normally, the writer or publisher doesn't receive any kind of money for holds. I've only once heard of a publisher talking a record company out of a pretty good chunk of money for the label to hold a song. Don't ever count on this happening. I still don't know how the publisher pulled that off.

Most publishers, writers, and song pluggers treat holds as fairly sacred. If they tell someone they will hold a song, they will generally stay true to their word. However, some will still pitch the song that's on hold to try and get second, third, and fourth backup holds in case the first one falls through and gets passed on.

Better yet, sometimes a writer gets a call that lets him know a "big-name artist" loves one of his songs, and is cutting it or recording it tomorrow. Nobody would mind having their dinner interrupted for a call like that, would they? However, even with this kind of news, you still can't be sure that it's a done deal.

First off, the artist, record label, producer, or anyone else in the song selection process could change their mind by tomorrow. Worse yet, someone else could bring in a last-minute pitch or song that bumps the song that was scheduled to be recorded.

Assuming that the song didn't get bumped and really did get recorded, it's still not in the bag. Sometimes artists will "over cut," or record, say, fifteen songs, knowing they'll have to narrow it down to as few as ten. This means that as many as five songs that are recorded will not make the final ten-song CD. The old saying (from back before cassette tapes and CDs) was "It ain't final 'til it's vinyl." For you young whippersnappers, vinyl is the material that old records or albums were made from. It's funny that even today the terms "record" and "album" are still commonly used to refer to a project that will ultimately be released on CD or cassette tape.

The moral of all of this is that "holds" and "cuts" are extremely good things, but bad things can still happen. Many writers have learned the hard way not to celebrate until their song is included on a shrink-wrapped CD in Wal-Mart's music section.

Singles are even worse. When someone tells a writer that one of his songs is going to be a single selected for radio airplay, especially if they say first single, it's kind of like the kiss of death. I can't tell you how many times writers have been devastated when news like this didn't turn out to be true.

A good friend of mine, Robert Arthur, with fourteen major label cuts by artists including Brad Paisley, Mark Chesnutt, and Daryle Singletary, has experienced one of the worst *now you've got a single, now you don't* stories I've ever heard. Robert and his cowriter had been told for weeks that they had a single coming out on a very successful major label act. In fact, they had even seen the title of their song in a popular trade publication with the release date right beside it. Sounds like a sure thing, doesn't it? Keep reading.

Six days before the release date of the single, Robert got a call from his publisher. Reluctantly, Robert's publisher told him that the record label had changed its mind and was going with a different song for the single. *How close can you get?* Check this out. The record label had *already pressed* the CD single of Robert's song and shipped it out to radio land. Sadly, Robert still has his copy of the CD single that got all the way into the hands of radio but never got played. He was six days away from having a single that could have changed his life financially and career-wise.

Robert says that he has lost singles in every possible way they could be lost. He's even been next in line for the "for sure next single" of a successful artist, and had to suffer through watching the record label scrap the whole project because of an upcoming merger. The artist lost his record deal and once again, Robert lost his single.

Another thing that is mostly out of writers' control is who records their songs. A publisher or song plugger can pitch songs to any artist they choose. Remember, the publisher owns the songs, not the writer. Usually, the publisher wants to get the songs to the most popular or biggest-selling artists, but this doesn't always happen. Sometimes a publisher takes a chance by pitching a writer's best song to a new act that is unknown and unproven. *This gamble can pay off big!* Remember, Garth Brooks, Alan Jackson, and George Strait were once unknown and unproven. I know some writers who are glad their publisher took that chance. However, a gamble like this can come up snake eyes and everyone loses. For example, some new artists just aren't received well by radio. Their first single may never even crack the Top 40. If the single flops, there's no sense in putting out the record because no one is going to buy it. Worse still, some new artists record entire albums that no one ever hears. These don't even get a shot at radio. The record label keeps pushing back the release date, for whatever reason, until the label finally decides to can the whole project and drop the act altogether. Think of all the time that is wasted with what may be a writer's best song!

But if this happens, it's not the end of the world—even though it may feel like it at the time. Nothing says that some other artist can't record the same song later. Your song may live to play another day.

Publishers have a say about who records a song the first time, but not about who records it thereafter. A publisher could deny or refuse to issue a mechanical license to a record company, and then the record company could not record and release the song to the public. However, once the publisher has issued a mechanical license or has given permission to someone to record a song, then anyone can record that song whether the publisher wants them to or not. At this point, the publisher issues what is known as a compulsory license to whoever wants to record the song. Even though the publisher no longer has control over who records the song, the publisher is still entitled to mechanical royalties.

Another factor that adds to the sometimes exhilarating, sometimes nauseating, roller-coaster ride of being a full-time songwriter is the short time provided to prove oneself. It is not uncommon for writers to have contracts with an initial term of one year. This normally is followed by one to four additional one-year option periods. These option periods give the publisher the option to keep the signed writer under contract for an additional year.

As you can see, the writer is under tremendous pressure to produce quality songs and somehow manage to get some excitement going with her songs in a relatively short amount of time. This is not to say that if a writer doesn't get a cut in the first year, she is automatically let go. But the writer had better have started at least getting some real bites. The publisher needs to be able to see success in the future based on what the writer is turning out right now.

A staff writer also has to spend a great deal of time establishing and maintaining relationships. This can involve business lunches, dinners, after-hour showcases, and various writers' nights. Though this type of networking is important for veteran writers, it is especially important for writers who are in their first deal. Talent is one of the most important parts of success, but being known and liked doesn't hurt.

Another negative disguised as a positive is that full-time songwriters are self-employed. Being your own boss has many pluses but also many minuses—the biggest of which is dealing with taxes. Self-employment can seem very expensive. Publishers don't withhold taxes from writers' payments, so the writers have to pay the taxes an employer would normally deduct from a paycheck. Suddenly that check doesn't look nearly as big. Did I mention that most songwriters don't get any benefits? That's right: if you want medical and dental insurance, it's going to cost you.

The plus side of self-employment is that you can deduct expenses you have incurred in pursuit of your profession, and this can make a huge difference in how much tax you owe. Check with your friendly tax planner, or buy a good computer tax program such as TurboTax Home & Business. *(Yep, the cost is tax deductible.) Be sure to save all your receipts for anything associated with your songwriting, and keep track of mileage.*

Anyway, most songwriters pay taxes quarterly. These estimated quarterly payments should total the amount of taxes that will be due for the year. Generally, you base this on the amount you paid the previous year. Any shortcomings will have to come out of your pocket on April 15—and if you've misjudged your income and underpaid those estimated taxes, you may even have to pay a penalty.

Well, I'm hoping you've learned that being a full-time songwriter is not just about sleeping in and avoiding rush hour traffic by a couple of hours. Though the crap factor is well below the national average, it does still exist. And though writers are technically self-employed, most of them expect more and put more pressure on themselves than any employer possibly could.

CHAPTER 13

SO WHAT IS A MUSIC PUBLISHER LOOKING FOR?

I can't seem to get a straight answer.

MUCH LIKE POLITICIANS, MUSIC PUBLISHERS ARE notorious for giving vague answers to direct questions. Here are a few answers you would likely get if you were to directly ask a publisher the question, "So what kind of songs are you looking for?"

- "Hits."
- "Something with a great groove."
- "Something really unique."
- "Something fresh."
- "I'll know it when I hear it."

That's not a great deal of direction, is it? However, as frustrating as those answers can be, as far as the publisher is concerned, the question is equally as frustrating. The one and only thing that publishers will continually be looking for is a hit song. It is up to the writer to come up with that hit song.

Now I'm not saying that publishers can't give their writers insight as to what artists, producers, and record labels are looking for, because they can and do. Publishers get the scoop and spread the news to their writers. After all, they want their writers to have every possible chance of getting their songs recorded, because the publisher stands to benefit just as much, if not more, when and if their writers are successful.

Publishers are flooded with appointments, tapes, and CDs from potential new writers eager to get signed. Making a decision about whom to and not to sign is never easy. There's a great deal of talent out there. As strange as this sounds, it seems that some publishers look for every reason not to sign a writer. You must keep in mind that, depending on the size of the publishing company, the writer and the company's employees will probably be spending a fair amount of time together. For this reason, the publisher doesn't want to sign a writer who's going to be a constant thorn in everyone's side. Bad attitudes and cynical views of the business send bad vibes to the publisher, and those bad vibes can come back as bad news to a writer who finds himself out of a deal.

Some publishers, however, don't give a squat about company harmony. They go after the writers whom they feel will monetarily benefit the company the most. Even if they can't stand the writer, they'll hug and smile like family at the Number 1 parties and award shows. It should also be noted that especially at bigger publishers, the staff and the writers really don't bump into each other that often.

Do you remember how we talked about the importance of relationships? From the publisher's side of the desk, a writer's relationships can be a key ingredient. Writers who are "plugged in"—who have lots of contacts or know people in positions of influence—are extremely attractive to publishers.

There are two ways that a writer can be plugged in. One is having a strong list of cowriters, and the other is being well connected to other important people in the music industry.

Let's talk about cowriters first. If a writer who has never been signed to a publishing deal has managed to get aligned with writers who do have publishing deals, that is a definite plus. It's even more advantageous if these "bigger writers" have had songs recorded or, better yet, have had or currently have singles on the radio. The more successful an unsigned writer's cowriters are, the better. The publisher knows that a young or unsigned writer stands a better chance of getting cuts by having his or her name on songs with more successful writers than by writing alone or with virtually unknown cowriters.

Finding that a new writer is already well connected in the music industry is also attractive to a publisher. Sometimes these writers have somehow developed relationships with various artists, producers, managers, A&R reps at record labels, and so on. From the publisher's point of view, writers like this may very well be able to help get their own songs recorded by using the relationships they have already developed.

Though it is a tremendous advantage, being plugged in is not the only way for an unknown writer to land a publishing deal. When I got my first publishing deal, I wasn't plugged in at all. The publisher obviously believed I had potential to become a successful songwriter, but potential was all I had at the time. I had just graduated from Belmont University and had very few contacts or cowriters. To be honest, I'm quite sure that I got my first publishing deal based mostly on the fact that the people at the publishing company liked me. My ego would feel better if I could tell you it was because of my one-of-a-kind talent and that the publisher signed me before some other lucky company did. However, that simply wasn't the case.

I had interned at that small publisher for more than a year doing mostly what the paid employees didn't want to do. In a way, I guess I had made myself indispensable. They knew that if they didn't hire me after graduation, I'd have to look for work elsewhere, forcing them to go back to doing all the things they had gotten used to me doing. (I love it when a good plan comes together.)

Because the publisher believed I had potential as a writer and also wanted me to continue doing the office work that I had been doing, I was hired as a full-time employee and signed as a part-time writer on the same day. Because I had become very interested in the business side of music publishing as well, this setup suited me just fine. Besides, I was offered only $10,000 a year to write songs. That's gross, not net. So I worked in the publishing office from nine to five to earn an extra $14,000 a year and then wrote songs every night after work until it was time to go to bed.

Not until three years later did I land my first full-time writing deal. This time it had everything to do with the fact that I was more plugged in. I had been running a small publishing company called Music Alley. Though only a small company with four writers, including me, it was a huge opportunity. I was able to sign and help develop writers and expand my contacts exponentially. Over time, I had gotten to know several record company A&R reps, artists, producers, managers, and so on because I was always calling them and pitching them songs from our catalog. It was also during this time that I was just beginning to have some success as a songwriter myself.

When approaching EMI Music Publishing in hopes of obtaining a position as a staff writer, I felt confident that EMI would be interested. Again, it wasn't that I believed I was the greatest writer in the world. It was that I had something to offer. At that time, I had just recently gotten my first cut on Tracy Byrd's album. Though my previous publisher, Music Alley, already owned this song, it at least showed that I was a writer who was beginning to have some song activity. This, coupled with the fact that I also had a David Ball cut and two cuts on Brad Paisley's record, was enough to entice EMI into offering me a deal. The enticing part of these cuts for EMI wasn't just that I had cowritten them, but that my publishing portion of these three particular songs was open. Songs that are open are songs that no one, other than you, owns the publishing rights to. In other words, the publishing is up for grabs.

Can you see why this scenario was attractive to EMI? I was asking for a full-time publishing deal in which EMI would pay me in the form of advanced royalties for my writing services. This was attractive to EMI because I was willing to assign or sign over the copyright or ownership on three songs that had already been recorded, instead of EMI signing me hoping that I would get songs recorded some time in the future. Do you see the beauty of it for the publisher? Did EMI have anything to risk here at all? You bet! Some time after signing the deal, we learned that the David Ball cut didn't make the final project. That means it never made it to Wal-Mart. Furthermore, Brad Paisley's record hadn't been released yet. Though everyone believed in Brad's project, no one knew for sure that it would be as successful and have as much critical acclaim as it did. It paid off for EMI, but what about me?

I've had several people tell me that I was crazy for signing over the ownership on those three cuts to EMI. They say I could've made twice the money if I had kept them myself. Could I have made twice the money by keeping the songs and maintaining ownership in the copyrights? Yes, I could've made exactly twice as much. However, if I'd kept the songs, I probably wouldn't have gotten the writing deal—at least not the writing deal I wanted. Being able to bring those songs into the deal made it all make sense for EMI. Did EMI acquire songs that were already cut and reap the benefits without doing anything to get them recorded? Yes, but let's look at what it did for me.

EMI advanced me enough money to support my family and to support my dream of being a full-time songwriter. Without this financial support, I wouldn't be free to write songs for a living. I would also have to spend eight to fourteen hours a day at some other job I don't enjoy nearly as much. If I'm at work all day doing something else, what does that mean I'm not doing? You guessed it: writing. If I'm not writing every day, what am I not getting? I'm not getting any better. How can I truly continue to grow as a writer unless I am free in every way to focus all my energy and efforts on writing? Here's the way I look at it. Since signing over the rights to those three initial songs, I've had several other songs recorded by successful acts. Could this have happened if I had been pursuing a writing career only in my spare time? *No way!* Furthermore, I wouldn't have song pluggers out there on Music Row right now trying to get my songs recorded to help advance my career.

Many writers have the attitude that publishers always want something for nothing. I totally disagree. I do feel, however, that they want as much as possible for as little as possible. Now let me ask you this: What profitable business that aims to stay in business doesn't? This is not to say that you should sell yourself short. Keep in mind that publishers need great writers just like great writers need publishers. If you have something to offer, you may be amazed at what they offer you.

An exclusive writing deal is not easy to come by. Occasionally, a writer will come to town with material that is already great. This person won't have much of a problem finding an interested publisher. This can happen, but it's fairly rare and unique.

In many cases, a writer has to have at least one of his songs recorded by a major artist before a major publisher will even consider that writer. However, sometimes a smaller publisher will sign a writer based on potential. The publisher believes that the writer has the necessary skills and, with some fine-tuning, the potential to become a huge success. Larger publishing companies, however, seem to prefer to sign writers who can produce immediate results. This is not always the case, but for the most part, it seems to hold true.

Song Pluggers

Are they really that important?

A SONG PLUGGER, YOU MAY REMEMBER, IS SOMEONE in the creative department of a publishing company who pitches writers' songs to anyone who will listen (anyone connected to an artist on a major record label, that is). Some smaller publishing companies have only one plugger, while larger companies have two, three, four, and sometimes even more. Their responsibilities vary from company to company, but one thing stays the same: a song plugger can be a writer's best friend.

For most writers, a song plugger is their only hope of ever getting their songs recorded at all. Most writers don't have the kind of connections necessary to place their own songs. For instance, not all writers are fortunate enough to have relationships with artists, producers, and so on, making it almost impossible for them to effectively pitch their own material. Therefore, they are totally dependent on the plugger for their success.

Sometimes good song pluggers are present during every stage of the songwriting process. They make themselves readily available to their writers so that the writers can bring them songs in their most raw state. After listening to a new song, a plugger can sometimes offer suggestions to help strengthen it. Not all song pluggers have a good song sense (the ability to analyze songs and offer helpful criticism). On the other hand, some have an incredible song sense and can really help develop the talent of writers. More times than I can remember, a plugger has given me or my cowriters sound advice that helped take a song to the next level.

Pluggers are out there on the front lines pitching songs against incredible odds. Their reputation is at stake with each song they pitch. This is why some pluggers are extremely picky about what they pitch. If they pitch weak or substandard material, they are the ones who appear not to know a good song from a bad one. This is a plugger's nightmare. If pluggers get a reputation for not knowing songs, then they won't have a lucrative or lasting career. When artists, producers, record labels, and managers are looking for hit songs, they usually turn to pluggers who have brought them hits in the past.

Many of the song pluggers I know and work with are extremely passionate about what they do. In fact, sometimes some of them are more passionate about songs than the writers. It's kind of like they are pitching their own songs, because they get so close to them.

Good pluggers also really help songwriters by alleviating the pressure of networking. After pluggers put in a good day's work at the office, developing writers and going to pitch meetings, they don't normally head straight home. They are constantly going out at night to showcases, writers' nights, sporting events, and parties. Sounds like a blast, right? Well, in a way it is, and in a way it isn't. Though they get to do a lot of fun stuff, they constantly have to be "on." Even after hours they are still on the clock, so to speak. They continually have to maintain old and develop new relationships with heavy hitters in the music industry. This can be very tiring, and it's a never-ending battle to stay on top of their game. So where do you think the songwriters are while the pluggers are doing all this networking? Most of us are at home with our families.

So far we have been talking about song pluggers who are employed by music publishers. However, there is another kind of plugger known as an independent song plugger. These pluggers are not tied to a publisher at all. They choose what writers or publishers they want to represent. Some charge a monthly or quarterly fee, while others require that the writer or publisher give up a portion of the publishing percentage on the songs the plugger gets recorded. The advantage is that an independent plugger can usually give your catalog of songs more individual attention than at a publishing company, where your catalog is "competing" with a bunch of other writers. The disadvantage is that there are no guarantees. Nothing contractually says the plugger must get your songs recorded. If you're paying cash money, this can get expensive, especially if there are no results.

There's nothing wrong with hiring an independent song plugger. In fact, even though I have a publishing deal, I have tried this a few times in the past. Though I have never gotten a cut through an independent, many writers have. My publisher has been doing a great job pitching my material lately, and I haven't found it necessary to seek outside help. If I ever hire an independent again, I will spend a considerable amount of time researching the plugger's track record. If a plugger has never gotten anyone a cut, that usually means one of two things. Either the plugger doesn't really have any contacts or has been pitching mediocre songs—or it could be a combination of the two. Either way, I would find someone who has had proven success.

Good independent song pluggers will also be selective about whom they represent. They normally won't pitch a writer's songs if they don't believe in them, even if the writer offers to compensate them nicely. If pluggers agree to pitch substandard material, they run the risk of damaging their own credibility. If they lose credibility, it will be next to impossible to continue to set up pitch meetings. If they can't get meetings, they can't get songs heard. If they can't get songs heard, they will lose all their clients. If they lose all their clients, they won't have any money to operate.

So you see, it's not only writers who have to be careful whom they associate with. The plugger has to be careful as well.

CHAPTER 15

CONTRACTS

Can't live with 'em, can't work without 'em.

AS WE MENTIONED A FEW CHAPTERS BACK, IF A publisher feels that you have written a hit song, that publisher may be willing to hire professional studio musicians to record your song in a music studio. If a music publisher does decide to put money into a professional demo, the publisher most likely will ask you to sign a "single-song contract." By doing this, you are giving the publisher the rights to the song and the right to exploit your material. Remember, *exploit* is a good word here! This means the publisher will do everything in its power to get your song recorded by a major recording artist, and *this can mean bucks!*

I know you're thinking there has to be a catch. After all, I've basically just told you that if a publisher wants to demo one of your songs, it won't cost you a dime. Is it *really* free? Let's just say it's free for now. By paying the initial cost of the demo, the publisher is actually advancing you royalties. If the song does get "cut" or recorded by an artist, either half or all the demo costs will be recouped (or deducted) from the royalties you earn. (Whether half or all of the demo costs are recoupable depends on the terms of your specific single-song contract.) It's even possible that the demo costs won't be recoupable at all, but that's highly unlikely.

Normally, you would be required to pay the publisher back only when an artist records your song. If an artist never records your song, you won't owe the publisher a dime. It's not like a debt owed to a credit card company—there is no accruing interest! You don't have to pull any money out of your own pocket. Only the publisher is at risk here. Once again, this too depends on the terms of the contract. If a major act does record your song, you will barely notice the few hundred dollars deducted from your thousands in royalties to pay the publisher back for the demo cost. I don't think any of us would mind that at all.

Someone once asked me, "If I sign a single-song contract, does that mean I would be writing solely for that publisher?" *No!* A single-song contract is a contract for one particular song. If you sign a contract of this nature, you are assigning the copyright of this one song to the publisher. This means the publisher now owns the song. It is no longer yours. Once again, this is not a bad thing. Your name will still be on the song, and you will still receive all of the royalties that you, as the writer, are entitled to. Not to mention the fact that without a publisher, your chances of getting a song cut are slim to none. Have you ever heard the saying, "I'd rather have 50 percent of somethin' than 100 percent of nothin'"? It certainly applies here. Further, you are not tied down to this one publisher, as the publisher owns the rights to only that one contracted song. You are free to pitch or play all of your other songs to any publisher in the world.

Some may think that with this being the case, maybe they should try to sign as many single-song contracts as possible. Though I can see the short-term logic, let me tell you why I think that is an incredibly bad idea. Though you may have to start out by signing a couple of these contracts here and there, you don't want to have all of your songs tied up this way. You need to be saving some of your songs so that you can try to land an exclusive songwriting deal. In other words, you will probably need to have a few unsigned songs to bring to the table for a full-time publishing deal.

So what do you do if a publisher does want you to write solely for its company? Please pay close attention here so that if you're confronted with this situation, you'll know exactly what to do first. Are you ready? Okay, the first thing you want to do is breathe. Then, call all of your family, friends, and enemies and tell them that you won't forget about them when you become rich and famous.

All right, I guess we better answer the business part of this question. If a publisher does want you to write solely for that company, you would be asked to sign an exclusive songwriting contract. This means that every song you write, for the entire term of the contract, belongs to that publisher. More often than not, you will also have to sign over all songs not previously signed to another publisher. The songs that you bring in to the deal, as we've mentioned before, are collectively called your Schedule A.

Most writers refer to signing an exclusive contract as "having a deal." They may also say that they have just been "signed"—and now they are no longer "unsigned." In short, the writer has a publishing deal or an exclusive songwriting agreement with a major publishing company. A writer with this type of contract may also be referred to as a staff writer.

Whether you're considering signing a single-song contract or an exclusive songwriting agreement, know who you are signing with. Is it a viable publisher? Has this publisher ever had songs recorded by artists on major record labels? Don't be afraid to ask questions. You're not going to blow the deal by making certain that you are signing with a legitimate publisher who actually has the power and connections to get your songs recorded. If you do blow the deal by asking pertinent questions relevant to the well-being of your career, then you know you were in the wrong place to begin with.

I'm also not sure how advantageous it would be to sign with a publishing company in a town or city where there is not really a music scene. I would really do some research in cases such as these. As many of you know, Nashville is not the only music or songwriting community. Los Angeles, New York, Austin, Memphis, and even Atlanta all have music communities. However, these music communities, with the exception of Austin, probably aren't ideal locations to pursue country music. But a person who writes pop, rap, or blues may be better advised to begin a search in these other areas. Not that it's impossible to get songs recorded in other genres of music if you write in Nashville. It's not uncommon for a contemporary-sounding "country" song to cross over into the pop market. A couple of examples are Lonestar's "Amazed" and Leann Womack's "I Hope You Dance." It seems to be a given that huge songs like these will achieve success on the pop charts because they have a pop flavor and have already enjoyed incredible success on the country charts.

If you're a Nashville writer, however, and your primary goal is to achieve success in the pop market, then I would say that you're in the wrong place. I'm not saying that it can't happen here, but it won't be easy. Some Nashville publishing giants obviously have connections to New York or L.A. However, the Nashville offices seem to be primarily focused on getting cuts in the country music market.

On the flip side, several pop writers from L.A. and New York have been successful in the country music market over the last few years. While some of these writers come to Nashville only every now and then to pitch their material, others have actually moved here to cash in on "country" since it has become "less country" in recent years. I believe that a pop writer stands a much better chance of getting a country cut than a country writer stands of getting a pop cut.

Finally, whether you're considering signing a single-song contract or an exclusive songwriting agreement, *hire an attorney!* Preferably one well versed in the workings of the music business and entertainment industry law. There are no ifs, ands, or buts about this one. Spend the money now, because it will save you later in more ways than one.

CHAPTER 16

SHOW ME THE MONEY!

Advanced royalties, mechanical royalties, and what's a royalty?

EARLIER WE BRIEFLY DISCUSSED HOW MOST SONG-writers are just a hair different from everyone else. Well, we don't even get paid like everyone else. In fact, some don't get paid at all. When talking to aspiring songwriters, one of the first questions to come up is almost always about the money. So let's talk about it.

I guess the first question that needs to be addressed is, "Do writers signed to exclusive deals get a paycheck?" There's a simple answer to that question: no and yes, but probably not how you think. I'll admit that doesn't look as simple on paper as it sounded in my head, but it will clear up in a minute. The fact is, whether writers get compensated for their services depends completely on the terms of the agreement.

Certainly some writers signed to exclusive publishing deals do not receive any form of payment up front. Now, this doesn't necessarily mean that these writers are less valuable than the writers who do get paid on the front end. There could be a number of reasons for this setup. More times than not, the music publisher is extremely small and can't afford to pay out anything until income from recorded songs starts to come in. Or a publisher may sign a young or developing writer because someone sees some raw potential in this person. The publisher doesn't feel that the writer is ready to be writing full time, but wants to work with him and develop his talent. Most of the time, the publishers in these scenarios will front money to cover the demo costs during the term of the contract, but that's about the extent of their financial obligation. So until future royalties are a present reality, songwriters signed to this sort of deal can't really afford to quit their day job.

What about those writers who do get a paycheck? Many Nashville songwriters who have publishing deals do get a paycheck, and the better the writer, the bigger the check. Of course, some of the more successful writers don't want a big paycheck or a paycheck at all because, in a sense, they are borrowing their own money. Others need the money up front and don't care whose money they are borrowing.

Let me explain. These checks we're talking about aren't exactly like the paycheck you may be bringing home now. A publisher pays an exclusive writer in the form of "advanced royalties." Say, for instance, that a staff writer named Bubba receives a $400 weekly "draw" or advanced royalties for his writing services. Let's also assume that his publisher has great contacts in the music industry and gets one of Bubba's songs recorded by a major label superstar named Doug C. Mandeville. Doug is signed to Almost Records, an extremely successful major record company. (In case you haven't guessed it, Doug C. Mandeville and Almost Records are fictitious names.) Anyway, let's say that Almost Records sells a million copies of Doug Mandeville's record, which includes the song that Bubba wrote. In this case, Bubba and his publisher have done extremely well. Both parties are now entitled to mechanical royalties, royalties from record sales.

The statutory rate for mechanical royalties as of January 1, 2002, set by the Copyright Royalty Tribunal in Washington, is eight cents per unit or record sold. Currently, this rate is up for review every couple of years. Though the rate for mechanical royalties is already ridiculously low, it can sometimes be negotiated even lower. Some record clubs and the like normally negotiate what is referred to as a reduced statutory rate, usually 75 percent of the full rate. Songs that are part of compilation CDs (a collection of various songs) may also be granted a similar rate. Publishers can stand firm and refuse the reduced rate, but not many do. The reasoning is that 75 percent of something is better than 100 percent of nothing.

Many record companies refuse to pay the statutory rate for mechanicals on CDs and tapes that include more than ten songs. Their refusal is based on the fact that the more songs there are on an album, the more money they have to pay out to publishers and writers. This, of course, would mean less profit for the record company. Most of the time this comes into play when the recording artist is also a songwriter. Some artists have been known to give up their mechanical royalties on a song or two just so they will be allowed to put more than ten songs on their CD.

Now let's figure out Bubba's situation.

The first thing we want to do is to multiply the mechanical royalty rate of eight cents (or $0.08) by one million units sold to determine the gross figure due to Bubba and his publisher.

$$\$0.08 \times 1,000,000 = \$80,000$$

Wow! Not bad, right? In most cases, since Bubba is a new writer, he and his publisher split this right down the middle: 50 percent for Bubba and 50 percent for his publisher.

$$\$80,000 \div 2 = \$40,000$$

Bubba and his publisher both just made more off one song than many folks make in a whole year. Normally, however, it would take anywhere from nine to fifteen months after the commercial release of the record for Bubba and his publisher to receive most of this income. The money from the record buyers or consumers, on its way back to the record company, is in the pipeline and takes a while to arrive. The record companies also hold a certain percentage of income in reserves to cover returns.

Okay, a year passes and Bubba's publisher receives a check from Almost Records for $80,000. In some cases, an administration company would be responsible for collecting these royalties from the record company and then, after deducting a small percentage, would forward the remaining balance to the publisher. Anyway, once the publisher receives the check, it immediately takes its half share of the $80,000, which is $40,000. This leaves $40,000 for Bubba, right? *Wrong!*

Remember when we said that Bubba has been receiving advanced royalties in the amount of $400 a week? Well, those advanced royalties are exactly what the term implies. This is money the publisher advances to the writer in hopes that it will be fully recouped (or paid back) once major artists record some of the writer's songs.

Now that Bubba has had a song recorded by Doug Mandeville, he has some paying back to do. Let's say that by the time Bubba's publisher received the $80,000 royalty check, Bubba has been receiving his $400 a week for exactly two years. There are 52 weeks in a year, so he has been drawing this check for 104 weeks.

$400/week x 104 weeks = $41,600

Bubba's publisher has already paid him more than the $40,000 the Doug Mandeville cut earned—so Bubba owes his publisher all of these royalties and then some.

It may sound complicated, but it's really pretty simple. Bubba's song earned $80,000. His publisher gets half, and Bubba has to "pay back" all of his weekly advance before he gets to pocket any more money. In short, the publisher has every right to recoup or pay himself back by deducting the cost of Bubba's weekly draw for those two years from Bubba's earned royalties.

In addition, Bubba owes his publisher $350, half the cost of the demo that enabled Bubba to get his song recorded by Doug Mandeville in the first place. This $350 is also recoupable, so Bubba actually owes his publisher the $41,600 from his weekly paychecks plus $350, a total of $41,950. So, Bubba, unfortunately, doesn't get any extra money from this deal—and is still in the hole to his publisher for $1,950!

Hold on a minute. Do you mean to tell me that Bubba got one of his songs recorded by a huge artist like Doug C. Mandeville who then sold one million records, and he still owes money to his publisher? That's exactly right! Welcome to the music business.

Let's say, however, that Doug Mandeville's CD including Bubba's song had sold two million units! Then the income from the song would be

$$\$0.08 \times 2{,}000{,}000 = \$160{,}000$$

The publisher's share would be $80,000, and Bubba's share would also be $80,000. From this the publisher would subtract the $41,950 Bubba owes to "pay back" his salary for two years plus half the cost of the demo—and Bubba would take home the remaining $38,050. Not so bad, huh?

Keep in mind that we have only calculated how much Bubba receives off of record sales or mechanical royalties. We have yet to talk about the big money that comes from radio airplay. Read on!

CHAPTER 17

SHOW ME MORE OF THE MONEY!

And this time, bring it to my mailbox!

ALMOST RECORDS LIKES BUBBA'S SONG SO MUCH that it decides to release it as a single for radio airplay. *This is where the big money is!*

Let's assume that the song Bubba wrote becomes a Number 1 smash hit. Can you say *sweepstakes?* The money that Bubba and his publisher receive from radio airplay is called performance royalties, and to collect these royalties, they're going to need some help. They are in luck! Companies designed specifically for this type of service, you may remember, are called performing rights organizations (PROs).

One of the primary functions of these organizations is to collect performance royalties for writers and publishers. The three PROs you need to be familiar with are ASCAP, BMI, and SESAC, which we mentioned in Chapter 2. All three of these companies are continually searching for better ways to track the airplay of songs.

 Do you know how much a recording artist makes each time one of his or her records or CDs is played on the radio? Absolutely nothing. Can you believe that? The singer, provided he or she didn't write the song they are singing, doesn't get squat for radio performances. For an artist, radio is simply an advertising tool used to introduce listeners to their music in hopes that they will in turn drive to the record store and make a purchase of the song they heard on the radio. The artist is then compensated from record sales.

Radio airplay is not the only thing these companies keep up with. They are also responsible for collecting money for the public performance of music all over the United States. They have agreements with sister societies around the world that collect public performance income generated abroad. They can collect from almost every business establishment that uses music for such things as entertainment, atmosphere, or just pure listening enjoyment. If you've ever been to a dance club, a nightclub with a live DJ, a bowling alley, or even a Waffle House with a radio, odds are that these venues are paying ASCAP, BMI, and SESAC for the public performance of the music.

Let me back up just a minute and say that all this held much more water back before the infamous Restaurant Bill (now known as the Fairness in Music Licensing Amendment) was passed. This bill exempts many businesses from paying royalties.

So smaller venues such as the Waffle House now don't have to pay for the public performance of music, even though music is a big part of the Waffle House experience. By the way, I don't hold any special grudge against this establishment. In fact, I'm still a scattered, smothered, and covered kind of guy (for those of ya who ain't hip to the Waffle House lingo, this means hash browns with cheese and onions).

(text continues on page 122)

Why We Get Paid Even *Less* Now

The so-called Fairness in Music Licensing Amendment goes like this (this information is from the American Society of Composers, Authors, and Publishers' website, at www.ascap.com/legislative):

Businesses that perform music only from licensed radio, television, cable, and satellite sources; that do not re-transmit beyond their establishments; and do not charge admission, are exempted as follows:

- *All restaurants, bars, and grills that are smaller than 3,750 gross square feet, and all other retail establishments that are smaller than 2,000 gross square feet, are exempt from paying license fees to songwriters, composers, and music publishers, but only for their use of radio and TV music.*

- *Businesses whose square footage exceeds these amounts also qualify for the exemption if they use six or fewer speakers with no more than four speakers in any one room, or use audiovisual equipment consisting of no more than four TVs, with no more than one TV in each room, and no TV having a diagonal screen size greater than fifty-five inches, together with the same speaker restrictions. Copyright owners can recover penalties from the business owners if it is determined that their claims of exemption were frivolous.*

According to ASCAP, the Congressional Research Service estimates that more than 70 percent of restaurants and bars will be exempt from paying music license fees for radio and TV music.

It seems that the powers that be are saying if you're a small business, you don't have to pay for the public performance of music. You know, if the whole world operated that way, we'd be in a real mess, wouldn't we? All the short people would be going around demanding everything for free based on the fact that they are too small to have to pay. I know my analogy is ridiculous, but then again, so is the Fairness in Music and Licensing Act.

I think this is yet another way to keep songwriters from getting paid what they are due. I also think that the people who keep trying, and sometimes succeeding, to take income away from songwriters have no idea how little we make. To start with, we only get that eight cents per record sold, and we then split that with our publisher. That takes us down to four cents per unit sold. If we have a cowriter on the song, we're down to two cents per record, and if we have two cowriters, that would give us a whopping total of just a bit more than one shiny penny per record sold (1.33 cents).

Even if a writer does hit a good lick and gets a song released as a single to radio, that doesn't exactly make her rich. Even though she may make some really fat checks for a while, you have to keep in mind that this writer probably has been struggling for years. The bottom line is that writers need to be properly compensated for the work they do.

In the spring of 2002, I went with about fifty other songwriters to Washington, D.C., to talk to legislators about this very subject. We were trying to educate them and let them know why it is important that "would-be" consumers not be able to download our music for free. We will definitely be remembered. It's not every day that those folks see songwriters wearing suits and ties and carrying guitars. Thanks to Bart Herbison and the Nashville Songwriters Association International, the voices of songwriters are being heard all the way up on Capitol Hill.

Anyway, ASCAP, BMI, and SESAC generally collect from everyday businesses by issuing each of them a blanket license. This license grants venues the right to allow the public performance of all songs that are in the PRO's catalog for a flat fee, which is exactly what the term implies.

It is a fixed sum of money for a specified time period, which could be monthly or yearly. Anything is negotiable, and the fee is different for each music user. The size of the business, yearly income, and size of customer base are just a few factors that could affect the fee.

Each qualifying music-using venue has to pay a fee to ASCAP, BMI, or SESAC. These three companies are competitors, and each has its own catalog of songs. Now, this catalog of songs is not the same as the catalog of a music publisher. Unlike a publisher, neither ASCAP, BMI, nor SESAC own the songs. They merely grant performance licenses and collect performance royalties on behalf of the publishers and songwriters who have signed agreements with them. Just so you'll know, a writer can only be connected with one PRO at a time. For example, let's say that Bubba is a member of ASCAP. Therefore, ASCAP will collect all his performance royalties from his Number 1 hit song and any other songs he gets recorded, as long as he is a member. Since Bubba is a member of ASCAP and is the sole or only writer on the song, BMI and SESAC have no immediate interest in him or in any of his songs. If, however, Bubba had cowritten the song with a BMI writer, then BMI would have collected and distributed the cowriter's share of performance royalties.

What would happen if a business that publicly performs music decides only to pay BMI and SESAC? Are they forced to pay ASCAP also? No, but that business could not legally play any songs in ASCAP's catalog.

This would include the Number 1 smash hit that our good friend Bubba wrote. By not paying for licenses from all three of the PROs, businesses using music would miss out on a great deal of popular music. Most businesses that depend on the use of music for any reason cover themselves by paying fees and acquiring licenses from all three organizations. By doing this, they are free to play any song they want whenever they want, without wondering whether or not they are using music illegally.

Theaters in the United States usually are excluded from paying ASCAP, BMI, or SESAC for the use of music in a film. When a motion picture is being created, the selection of music is extremely important.

MOVIE MUSIC

Many factors determine how much money will be paid to artists, publishers, and writers for using their music in a motion picture. Some possible factors are:

- How important the song is to the movie
- How many times the song is played during the film
- If the song is played as background music, or if it is partly responsible for the success of a big scene
- If the whole song is played or just a few seconds of it
- If the artist that has made the song a hit is singing the song and is shown in the movie, or if we just hear a sound recording without the visual image of the artist

Remember, this is just a generalization. All things are negotiable, and each song is treated differently.

When the person in charge of music or song selection for a film decides on a particular song, he or she will contact the publisher or the publisher's administration company directly to request a synchronization license. This license allows the licensee (the entity who requested the license) to play music "in sync," or in time, with the motion picture.

The synchronization license pertains to television as well. For television, however, a flat fee normally is not used. The fee or royalty paid depends on how many stations broadcast the show containing the song.

In these situations, the PROs normally track the performances by requesting "cue sheets" or log sheets from each television station. This shows how many seconds or minutes of music are used during a program. The PROs also sometimes do random audio- and videotaping of network television to spot-check information provided by the networks.

Okay, back to Hollywood. As the folks in the motion picture industry deal either directly with publishers or their administration companies, they normally negotiate an upfront one-time fee for the use of the music. In short, the cost of the use of music is included in the expenses of the movie budget.

To finish up on ASCAP, BMI, and SESAC, let me say just a few things.

- They will not demo your songs.
- They normally will not pitch your songs.
- They will not copyright your songs.
- They are not music publishers.
- They do not collect mechanical royalties.

The criteria for becoming a member or an affiliate of ASCAP, BMI, or SESAC is different for each organization. Normally, you must have a record of a public performance of one or more of your songs, an exclusive songwriting agreement, or a single-song contract with a legitimate publisher. However, writers can sometimes sidestep these criteria by developing a good working relationship with one of the members or affiliate representatives at ASCAP, BMI, or SESAC.

If you are a writer who is getting airplay, being connected with one of these companies is an absolute must. It is virtually impossible to properly collect performance royalties without them.

Now, back to Bubba and his Number 1 single. Remember when we talked about Bubba still owing his publisher $1,950 for all of his advances despite having a song on a record that sold a million copies?

When we arrived at this figure, we had only been considering the earnings from record sales, which you now know are mechanical royalties. Here comes the good part! Bubba should receive anywhere from $175,000 to $275,000 for his Number 1 hit single on country radio, spread out over a four- to six-quarter period. Bubba would receive this huge chunk of change from ASCAP, because that is the PRO he belongs to. Have you caught your breath yet? Can you believe the money that can be made just by writing a great song?

 Earnings from radio play in other genres could vary significantly from country. For example, if Bubba's song had been Number 1 in the markets of pop, bluegrass, R&B, contemporary Christian, rap, or even polka, the amount of royalties earned would have been different. In other words, Bubba's checks would have been larger or smaller depending on the format, with pop earnings being the highest of the genres mentioned and polka probably the lowest.

It's amazing. Just a few minutes ago we had Bubba in a $1,950 hole. Now he's paying off his guitar and all his credit cards, and is in the process of building a house with a two- or maybe even three-car garage so he will have a place to keep his new paid-for bass boat and four-wheel drive utility vehicle. Again, welcome to the music business!

Do you know what the best part about this big money is? The best part of it is how it is delivered. Once every quarter Bubba is going to roll out of bed, stumble down the hall, trip over a few of his kid's toys, open the front door, step over the dog, walk to his mailbox, pull out an envelope from ASCAP, open it up, and then pee in his pajamas when he sees checks for $40,000, $60,000, $80,000 or $100,000. Oh yeah, Bubba's got mailbox money! The most-loved mail carriers in the world have to be the ones who deliver checks like this to hit songwriters.

Though the mailbox money gets smaller as time goes on, how long it lingers may surprise you. Some writers report that even after five years they make $8,000 to $12,000 annually off of an old Top 10 single. Can you believe that? Imagine if you had a few songs out there earning recurring income like that.

Have you ever heard of anyone selling a song? It's funny; sometimes when I go back home I'll run into someone I know and they ask, "Sold any songs lately?" Thank God, my answer is always no. Now that you see how much money can be made off a song, you can see it would be crazy to sell one for a one-time fee of, say, $500, or even $1,500. This happened somewhat frequently a long time ago, before writers like you took an interest in the business side of music and educated themselves.

By the way, Bubba will continue to get paid on this song every time it is played for the rest of his life, plus seventy years after he's dead and gone. This "Life + 70 years" comes from the Sonny Bono Copyright Term Extension Law. Isn't that great! Bubba could still be generating money for his wife, kids, and grandkids long after his earthly departure.

Okay, back to the living. Someone else will be equally as excited as Bubba, and that's Bubba's publisher. As the writer and the publisher get the same amount of performance royalties, his publisher also will receive a check from ASCAP for somewhere between $175,000 and $275,000 from Bubba's Number 1 hit. Even though Bubba is still a little in the hole as far as mechanical royalties are concerned, I'm sure his publisher is very happy with him. Overall, Bubba is way ahead financially, and in the eyes of his publisher, he's a hero. *Way to go, Bubba.* We're all very jealous of you. Did I say jealous? I meant to say proud.

The biggest difference between mechanical and performance royalties, in terms of recouping, is that normally the publisher can't touch the writer's portion of the performance royalties. Whatever amount the publisher gets, the writer gets, and whatever amount the writer gets, the publisher gets. However, this too depends on the terms of the writer's contract.

I can remember when the issue of publishers recouping writers' performance royalties wasn't an issue at all. It just wasn't a consideration. However, over the last couple of years, I've heard of several writers signing deals that allow a publisher to recoup performance royalties. Most of the time, a writer who signs a deal like this is a better singer than writer.

The publisher will sign the writer to a publishing deal and set him or her up with stronger writers to collaborate with. The intention of the publisher is to eventually land a record deal for this singer/songwriter.

If this happens, the publisher scores big time. A major label artist would then be writing for this publishing company. When the artist later goes in the studio to record a project, whose songs do you think he will record? Probably the same songs this artist has been cowriting with the stronger writers. The publisher now has a built-in outlet for getting songs recorded.

Another situation where a publisher may push to recoup a writer's performance royalties is if the writer is really green. In other words, the publisher signs the writer based not on what that writer can do today, but on what he might do in the future.

In either case, a publisher that requires a writer's performance royalties to be recoupable is simply trying to minimize the risk. If just one of the writer's songs gets cut and released as a single, the publisher quickly recoups the investment and then some. If a publisher can recoup expenses only from the writer's mechanical royalties, getting those expenses back could take a lot longer—or might never happen.

I will say this: even if I were a fresh, green writer, I would fight tooth and nail against signing away any of my performance royalties. It seems to me that it decreases your incentive if you feel you may perpetually be in the hole. A writer sometimes needs the dangling carrot of mailbox money to keep up morale. I would have to be extremely desperate before I would consider signing over my mailbox money in exchange for a publishing deal.

CHAPTER 18

THE IMPOSSIBLE

What are the odds of actually making it?

WHENEVER PEOPLE ASK ME WHAT I DO FOR A LIVING, it's always interesting to watch the expressions on their faces when I answer. The look could range anywhere from excited to sympathetic. More often than not, it's the latter. If you want to see that same compassionate look I'm talking about, tell someone that your dream is to become a hobo.

Unfortunately, that's the image of songwriters many people have. They believe only a chosen few actually make it, and everyone else is left to sleep in cardboard boxes and abandoned cars, warming their hands on cold winter mornings by holding them over fresh manure dropped by the horses of the mounted police. That's a nice visual there, isn't it?

Have you ever told anybody that you're a songwriter or that you want to become a professional songwriter? If you have, then you probably know what I mean. In all seriousness, it's like saying you've decided to become a professional lotto winner. Quite frankly, most people feel that you don't stand a chance and that the odds are stacked against you.

My friend Lee Miller and I wrote a song that was recorded and released as a single by a young country artist named Joe Nichols. We were excited about this song for several reasons. For one thing, it was the first single to ever be released off the new record label, Universal South, jointly headed up by industry giants Tim DuBois and Tony Brown. Another reason we were excited is that after only sixteen weeks it had already broken into the Top 20. The most important reason, for the purposes of this book, was the timing and the subject matter. The song was called "The Impossible," and the basic message of it was "Sometimes the things you think will never happen, happen just like that."

Can you see why I thought that this would be the most appropriate way to end this book? So many people think that becoming a successful songwriter is an unattainable goal. Some will go so far as to tell you that it is impossible. Are the odds against your landing a publishing deal? Without reservation, I must say they are not in your favor. Remember that supply and demand thing we talked about? The supply of songwriters looking for a deal is much greater than the demand. Hence, there are many songwriters without a deal.

You would think that it would be difficult only for new songwriters to find deals, wouldn't you? I'll let you in on a little secret. I know several songwriters who have had publishing deals who are now looking to be signed again. They are having just as much trouble, and sometimes more, than new writers. To say the least, the country music market has seen better days as far as record sales. When fewer records are being sold, publishers make less money. The less they make, the less they are able to invest in new and existing writers. This is not to say that it's easy to get signed when times are good, but in those good times publishers certainly are a little less skittish about signing writers.

The odds of getting a song recorded by a major label artist doesn't exactly make a rational person decide to move to Nashville and give it a go. Then again, who said songwriters are rational people? Seriously though, as many channels as a song has to go through, I'm still amazed that any song gets cut, much less released to radio as a single. I'm sure you've heard the expression, "too many chiefs, not enough Indians." Well, that's definitely the case on Music Row.

So is it true that only a chosen few songwriters actually make it? No. In fact, I don't even think that's a fair question. It's much too general. Here's how I think that question should be asked. Is it true that only a chosen few songwriters actually make it *big?* Now, that's a fair and answerable question. Yes, I do believe that only a handful of songwriters make it big. When I say big, I mean someone who's had so many cuts he can't readily tell you how many. This type of writer seems to have something on the charts almost constantly. It seems as if he can do no wrong. Some of them will even tell you they've had songs recorded that they didn't even feel were that well written. When you're hot, you're hot.

If you're wondering where I rank, let's just say that I know exactly how many of my songs have been recorded. I can't imagine ever having so many that I lose count, but this is exactly the point I'm trying to make. You don't necessarily have to be a phenomenon or a musical or lyrical genius to make it as a songwriter. Many songwriters just like me, for the time being, make a great living writing songs. You don't have to make it *big* to make it.

I'm positive that God doesn't make mistakes, so I think that He must have intentionally crossed a couple of wires when He made songwriters. The wires I'm talking about are the dream wires and the reality wires. We think that our dreams are reality and reality is our dreams. The reason I think He crossed them is so we wouldn't be able to tell the difference between the two. I guess that's why we never give up.

So there are really only a couple of choices here. You can either take what you've learned in this book and decide to somehow actively pursue your dreams or you can do nothing. No one can make that decision for you. If you saw the movie *The Rookie,* I bet you remember the scene where Dennis Quaid's character asks his father if he should go off to the big leagues. The father's reply goes something like this: "It's all right to dream about what you want to do, but there comes a time when you've got to do what you were meant to do." I think that can be taken positively or negatively, don't you?

I certainly can't tell you that it won't be difficult. However, I can say with certainty that it's not impossible. Writers are getting publishing deals, cuts, and singles every day. Why can't it be me? Why can't it be you? For all anyone knows, someone who's never even been to Nashville may have already written the best song the world has never heard.

About the Author

KELLEY LOVELACE WAS BORN IN PADUCAH, KENTUCKY, and grew up primarily in Hixson, Tennessee, on the outskirts of Chattanooga. He and his wife and son currently live in Franklin, Tennessee, just a few miles south of Nashville.

After basic training in the U.S. Army, Kelley received the Distinguished Honor Graduate Award as the top soldier in the company. He obtained the rank of specialist (E-4) during his two-year term of service at Fort Benning in Columbus, Georgia.

After graduating from Belmont University in Nashville, Kelley began working and writing at Larry Butler and Shug Baggott's music publishing company, Perdido Key Music. In two years he became president of this company and dubbed it Music Alley. He later landed a songwriting deal with EMI Music Publishing, where he continues to write songs full-time.

As a writer, Kelley has had more than a dozen songs recorded by artists Brad Paisley, Tracy Byrd, Teri Clark, David Ball, Mark Chesnutt, Clay Walker, Joe Nichols, and others. Among these recordings are four Top 20 Billboard hits:

"He Didn't Have to Be"/Brad Paisley   #1
(Brad Paisley/Kelley Lovelace)

"Wrapped Around"/Brad Paisley   #2
(Brad Paisley/Kelley Lovelace/Chris DuBois)

"Two People Fell in Love"/Brad Paisley   #4
(Brad Paisley/Kelley Lovelace/Tim Owens)

"The Impossible"/Joe Nichols   #10 and climbing!
(Kelley Lovelace/Lee Thomas Miller)

Kelley received Song of the Year nominations for "He Didn't Have to Be," cowritten and recorded by Brad Paisley, from the Country Music Association, the Academy of Country Music, and the TNN Music Awards. He was awarded Song of the Year for "He Didn't Have to Be" by the TNN Music Awards and *Music Row Magazine* and is coauthor of a gift book for stepfathers entitled *He Didn't Have to Be*. A made-for-television movie based on the same song is in the works.

As an active member of the Nashville Songwriters Association International, Kelley shares this group's vision of protecting the rights of songwriters worldwide. He joined them on a trip to Washington, D.C., to help inform legislators on how songwriters get paid and why stopping free downloading of music is important.

Kelley's hobbies are fishing, playing golf, weight training, jogging, dieting, reading, watching movies, and coaching Little League baseball. He is a deacon at Brentwood Baptist Church and is a supporter and facilitator of Search Ministries. He is active in ministry in his church and home, and on Music Row.

INDEX

A

A&R
  department, 20
  representative, 21, 32, 101
  defined, 11
Academy of Country Music, 134
Airplay
  foreign, 77
  radio, 119
    keeping track of, 120
    writers who are getting, 125
Album, defined, 95
Album cut, defined, 11
"Amazed," 112
American Society of Composers, Authors, and Publishers (ASCAP), 18, 22, 23, 119, 120, 123, 125, 126, 127
  contact information, 24, 25, 121
American Songwriter Magazine, contact information, 37
Andy Griffith (television program), lessons from, 81–82, 88
Antioch Bar and Grill, 45
Arista Records, 18
Arthur, Robert, 95
Artists
  avoid pitching songs to yourself, 64
  major, 104
  pitching songs to, 96
Artists and repertoire *see* A&R
ASCAP *see* American Society of Composers, Authors, and Publishers

Atlanta, 112
Attitude, keeping a good, 100
Attorney, need to hire, 112
Austin, 112

B

B songs, 86
Background vocals, defined, 10
Baggott, Shug, 133
Ball, David, 102, 103, 133
Bands, developing relationships with, 36
Belmont University, 13, 18, 24, 101
  address and contact information, 19
  offers degree in music business, 12
  requirements, 14
Berry, John, 74
BGV's, defined, 10
Billboard chart, 77
The Bluebird Cafe, 40, 45
Blues songwriting, 112
Blume, Jason, 25
BMI *see* Broadcast Music, Inc.
The Boardwalk Cafe, 45
Boss, being your own, 97
Bridge (song), defined, 60
Broadcast Music, Inc. (BMI), 22, 23, 119, 120, 123, 125
  contact information, 25
The Broken Spoke Cafe, 45
Brooks, Garth, 74, 75, 96
Brown, Tony, 130
Business administration, degree in, 18

Butler, Larry, 49, 133
Byrd, Tracy, 74, 102, 133

C

Catalog administration support, service provided by SGA, 22
CD burner, 55
CD Label Maker (software), 62
CD labels, 62, 64
  copyright information on, 65
CDs
  compilation, 77
    defined, 115
  cutting, 94
  medium of choice, 64
Charts
  Billboard, 77
  how far song goes on the, 43
  Radio & Records (R&R), 77
Chesnutt, Mark, 95, 133
Chord structures, simple, 17
Chorus (song), 60
Clark, Teri, 133
Collaboration, 11, 51
  see also Cowriting
Colleges
  costs of, 23
  a good starting place, 18
  that offer degrees in music business, 19
Commercial appeal, defined, 11
Commitment
  minimum, 91
  writer's, 90
Community college, financial savings by attending, 20
Competition, 30, 87
Compilation CD, 77, 115
Compositions, whole, 90
Compulsory license, 96
Constructive criticism, invaluable nature of, 83
Contacts
  establishing, 20
  having lots of, 100, 101
Contract(s), 109–112

exclusive, 111
single-song, 112, 125
  defined, 11, 109, 110
Control room, defined, 8
Copyright, 65–70, 110
  costs of, 66
  infringement, 69, 70
  notification methods, 65
  poor man's, 70
  registration process, 66
Copyright Office
  contact information, 66, 67
  filing an amendment with, 67
Costs, 23
  for copyright, 66
  for demos, 53, 54, 55, 56, 110
  for songs "on hold," 94
Country Music Association, 134
Cowriter(s)
  defined, 11
  locating, 22
  may be necessary, 17, 49
  optimum number of, 51
  well-connected, 101
Cowriting, 47–51
  successful, 48
"Crap" factor, 92
Creative director, 21
Credit, dividing by cowriters, 51
Criticism, constructive, 34, 83
Critique night, service offered by TSAI, 22
Cross over (music), 112
Cut(s), 95
  defined, 11, 110

D

Daily schedule, 92
Degree, music business, 21
Demo(s)
  about, 53–58
  costs of, 53–54, 55, 56, 110
  defined, 10
  full-blown, 56, 58
  sessions can be headache, 93
Demonstration recording *see* Demo

Desperation, pitfalls of, 78
Douglas Corner Cafe, 40, 45
Downloading, of music by consumers, 122
Dreams, songs from, 31
DuBois, Chris, 18
DuBois, Tim, 130
Dues
  of organizations, 23
  paying your, 1

E

Earnings *see* Money; Paycheck; Royalties
Education, of benefit to songwriter, 2
EMI Music Publishing, 18, 49, 102, 103, 133
Equipment, needed by songwriters, 54–55
Exclusive songwriting agreement, 125
  defined, 11
  hire an attorney to help with, 112
  not easy to come by, 104
Expenses, deducting, 97
Experience, on-the-job, 20
Exploit, good for publisher to do with songs, 109

F

Fairness in Music Licensing Amendment (Restaurant Bill), 120, 121, 122
Family, uprooting and effects on the, 29–30
Fees, 23
First Blood (motion picture), 5
Flexibility, needed by the writer, 32
Flying Saucer, 46
Form PA (Copyright Office), 66
Four-to-five-year rule, 40, 41
The French Quarter, 46
Full-time, writing, 47
Furniture, 91

G

Gill, Vince, 19
Goals, 41, 57
God
  blessings of talents from, 50
  and songwriters, 131
Graduates, college, 21
Guido's New York Pizzeria, 46
Guitar
  finding someone who plays, 16
  learning to play, 17
  tune before playing, 42
Guitar/vocal, defined, 10

H

Harmony, background vocals referred to as, 10
"He Didn't Have to Be," 50, 133, 134
Herbison, Bart, 122
Hit record, defined, 11
Hollywood, 125
Honesty, about your skills, 50

I

"I Hope You Dance," 112
"I Still Love the Night Life," 49
Ideas
  not copyrighted, 68, 69
  timing of, 31
  unique, 32
  writing down all, 32
"I'm From the Country," 49
"I'm Gonna Miss Her," 18
Image, of songwriters, 129
"The Impossible," 134
Impression, making a good first, 21
Instrument, ability to play, 16
Insurance, medical/dental, 97
Interns, student, 20
Internship programs, 20

J

J-card, 62, 64
  sample, 63
Jack Massey Business Center (Belmont University), 24
Jackson, Alan, 96
James, Tim, 36
Jesus, quote from, 43
Jones, George, 56

K

Keith, Toby, 38
Krasilovsky, M. William, 37

L

Lasater, Blake, 8
Lawyer, need to hire, 112
Legislative updates, by SGA, 22
License
  compulsory, 96
  mechanical, 96
  performance, 121, 123
  synchronization, 124
Licensee, defined, 124
Listener, important in song success, 87
Location (geographic), of songwriters, 27–34
Lonestar, 112
Los Angeles, 112
Lovelace, Karen, 14
Lovelace, Kelley
  about, 133–134
  early life, 3–9, 12
  first meeting with Nashville publisher, 82
  first publishing deal, 101
  full-time writing assignment, 102
  graduation from Belmont College, 49, 133
  writing successes of, 133–134
Lyric sheet
  copyright information on, 65
  folding, 62
  preparing, 60
  sample, 61
  typing, 62
Lyrics
  changing copyright information for, 67
  defined, 10
  finding music to go with, 17
  visual, 32

M

McCormick, David "Mac," 6
McCoy, Neal, 74
McEntire, Reba, 68
McGraw, Tim, 32, 77
Managers, 101, 106
MD recorder *see* Mini-disc recorder
Mechanical license, 96
Mechanical royalties, 10, 96, 114, 115, 125, 127
  defined, 10
Melody
  defined, 10
  needed along with good lyrics, 17
Melody patterns, simple, 17
Memphis, 112
Middle Tennessee State University, 13–14
  address and contact information, 19
  degree in recording industry, 18
  recording facility at, 19
Mike Curb School of Music Business (Belmont College), 18
Mileage, keep track of, 97
Miller, Lee, 130
Mini-disc recorder, 54, 55
Money
  wasting on recordings, 57
  writers and, 113–117
Montgomery, John Michael, 74
Moonlighting, 39
Motion picture industry, 123–125
Movies, music in, 123, 124
MTSU *see* Middle Tennessee State University
Music
  country, best locale for writers of, 112
  cross over, 112
  in motion pictures, 123
Music Alley (publishing company), 102, 133
Music business
  education and training for, 13–25
  geographic locations of, 27–34
  paying your dues in, 1
  terminology of, 10–11
Music publisher
  agreement with, 11
  defined, 10
  exclusive writing deal with, 104
  name of on lyric sheets, 60
  never pay for services from, 73
  owing money to, 116, 117

owns the songs, 96
and treatment of songs "on hold," 94
what they are looking for, 98–104
Music Row (magazine), 134
  contact information, 37
Music Row (Nashville), 12, 15, 28, 48, 104, 131
  colleges in proximity to, 19
  composed of tight groups, 85
  heart of entire music industry, 18
  misconceptions of, 79
  a world of its own, 44
Musicians
  finding, 16
  studio, 109
"My List," 38

N

Nashville
  close-knit groups in, 14
  closed-door town, 85
  greatness of, 44
  help for writers not living in, 35–36, 38
  moving family to, 29–30
  music business in, 1, 2
  needs songwriters, 88
  not only music community, 112
  not out to get you, 79
  pros of living in, 27–34
  where to perform in, 45–46
Nashville Music Guide (newspaper), 45
Nashville Scene (newspaper), 45
Nashville Songwriters Association International (NSAI), 21, 22, 23, 134
  on Capitol Hill, 122
  contact information, 24, 45
  regional workshops of, 35, 36
The Natural (motion picture), 4
Nervousness, 42
Networking
  with industry professionals, 28
  necessity for, 20
  by song pluggers, 106–107
New York, 112
Nichols, Joe, 133

NSAI *see* Nashville Songwriters Association International

O

"On hold," songs, 93, 94
"One of These Days," 32
Online search, for open mic venues, 46
Open mic nights, 40
  maximizing, 42–43
Open songs, defined, 102
Opinions, seeking out several, 58
Option periods, 97
"Over cut," 94
Overseas, getting your songs, 77

P

Paisley, Brad, 15, 18, 43, 95, 102, 133
  cowriting with, 49, 50
  publishing deal with EMI, 49
Parties, 106
Partners
  writing, 48
  see also Cowriters
Patience, a necessary virtue, 40
Paycheck(s), writers and, 113–117
Payments, 113–117
Perdido Key Music, 49, 133
Performance royalties, 119, 122, 123, 126, 127, 128
  collection of, 22
  defined, 10
Performance venues
  Antioch Bar and Grill, 45
  The Bluebird Cafe, 45
  The Boardwalk Cafe, 45
  The Broken Spoke Cafe, 45
  Douglas Corner Cafe, 45
  Flying Saucer, 46
  The French Quarter, 46
  Guido's New York Pizzeria, 46
  Tony Wade's Hall of Fame Lounge, 46
  12th and Porter, 46
Performing rights organization (PRO)
  defined, 10
  goals of, 22, 23, 119

Performing rights organization *(continued)*
  what they will not do, 125
    writer can belong to only one at a time, 123
Performing Songwriter Magazine, contact information, 37
Piano
  finding someone who plays, 16
  learning to play, 17
Piano/vocal, defined, 10
Pitch meetings, by song pluggers, 30–31
Pitch-a-Pro night, by TSAI, 22
Pluggers, song *see* Song pluggers
Poor man's copyright, 70
Pop songwriting, 112
Presentation, is everything, 59–64
Pride, songwriter's downfall, 84
PRO *see* Performing rights organization
Procrastination, 48
Producer(s), 21, 101
Publisher *see* Music publisher
Publishing contract review, service provided by SGA, 22
Publishing deal, defined, 11
Pull My Chain, 38

Q

Quaid, Dennis, 132
"Quota songs," 91

R

Radio
  songs released to, 87, 119
  see also Airplay, radio
Radio & Record chart, 77
Rap songwriting, 112
Raye, Collin, 74
Record (album), defined, 95
Record labels, 101, 106
Recorders, needed for demos, 54
Recording studio, 55
Redford, Robert, 4
Relationships
  establishing, 20
  importance of, 85, 100, 101

  new, 106
  unfruitful writing, 49
Relaxation, at open mic nights, 42
Restaurant Bill
  passing of, 120
  see also Fairness in Music Licensing Amendment
Restaurants, great places to moonlight, 39
Rights
  in open songs, 102
  signing over, 103
  see also Copyright
Rogers, Frank, 18
The Rookie (motion picture), 131
"Round Table" (BMI), 23, 25
Royalties
  advanced, 103, 110, 114
  collecting, 116
  difference between, 127
  mechanical, 10, 96, 114, 115, 125, 127
  performance, 10, 22, 119, 122, 123, 126, 127, 128
  writers and, 113–117
Royalty collection, service provided by SGA, 22
"Rumor Has It" (Clay Walker), 68
"Rumor Has It" (Reba McEntire), 68
Rushlow, Tim, 38

S

Sample J-card, 63
Sample lyric sheet, 61
Schedule, daily, 92
Schedule A, writer's, 72, 111
Schools, of music business, 13–14
Self-employment, 47, 97
SESAC (songwriter's organization), 22, 119, 120, 123, 125
  contact information, 25
SGA *see* Songwriters Guild of America
Sharks
  getting rid of them, 71–79
  those that prey on songwriters, 23
Shemel, Sidney, 37
Showcases, 106

Singers, hiring, 55, 56
Singing, Kelley's early attempts at, 8, 9
Singing ability, not needed by songwriter, 16
Single(s), 87, 95
  defined, 11
Single-song contract, defined, 11
Singletary, Daryle, 95
Skills, for open mic night, 42
Song evaluation service, 21
Song plugger(s), 21, 30, 51, 92, 96, 104
  defined, 11, 105
  importance of, 105–108
  independent, 107
  must like songs, 93
Song titles, 33
Song of Year (Country Music Association), 31
Songs
  "B," 86
  blues, 112
  commercial, 32
  discerning quality of, 58
  great, needed by newbie, 88
  hit
    looking for, 106
    writers must come up with, 100
  movie, 123, 124
  "on hold," 93, 94
  open, 102
  "over cut," 94
  parts of, 60
  pop, 112
  presentation of, 59–64
  pressure to produce quality, 97
  protecting, 65–70
  publisher owning of, 96, 110
  quantity versus quality, 83
  quota, 91
  rap, 112
  registering, 66, 67
  single, 87
  story behind, 42, 43
  type publishers looking for, 98–104
  weaker, 86

Songwriters
  disadvantaged, 84
  education of benefit to, 2
  full-time, 48, 89, 90–98
  hit songs needed by, 100
  image, 129
  musical skills needed by, 16–17
  needed by Nashville, 88
  owing money to publisher, 116, 117
  PROs and, 123
  relinquishing ownership of songs, 96
  supply greater than demand for, 130
  trade organizations for, 21–22
  types of, 84
  unsigned, 101
  where they live, 27–34
Songwriter's agreement, 47
Songwriters Guild of America (SGA), 22
  contact information, 24
Songwriting
  excitement of, 12
  odds of making it, 129–132
Space, for writing, 91
Sporting events, 106
Staff writer, 111
Stallone, Sylvester, 5
Starstruck Writers Group, 68
Statutory rate, 115
Story, behind the songs, 42, 43
"Straight Talk" (ASCAP), 23, 24
Strait, George, 96
Strength, knowing your, 50
Studio
  recording, 55
  time, booking, 93
Studio musicians, 109
Success, measuring, 27–28
Synchronization license, 124

T

Talent, 100
Taxes, 97
  paid quarterly, 98
Television, synchronization license for, 124, 125

Tennessee Songwriter Association
   International (TSAI), 22, 23
   contact information, 24
Terminology, music business, 10–11
This Business of Music (Shemel and
   Krasilovsky), 37
Time, for getting something going, 40, 41
Tip sheets, service offered by TSAI, 22
Titles, for songs, 33
TNN Music Awards, 134
Tony Wade's Hall of Fame Lounge, 46
Tools, writer's, 91
TSAI *see* Tennessee Songwriter Association
   International
Turbo Tax Home & Business, 97
12th and Porter, 46
"Two People Fell in Love," 134

V

Vassar, Phil, 74
Verses (song), 60
Vinyl, material of old records, 94
Visual lyrics, defined, 32
Vocals, background, 10

W

Walker, Clay, 68, 133
Weaknesses, knowing your, 50

Williams, Hank Sr., 6
Womack, Leann, 112
Wood, Jeff
   advice from, 78
   shark tale involving, 74–76
Work ethic, 90
Work tape, 57
Workshops, service provided by SGA, 22
"Wrapped Around," 133
Writers
   full-time, 48, 89, 90–98
   staff, 111
   see also Songwriters
Writers' nights, 106
Writer's room, a space for composing, 91
"Writers in the round," 40
"Writers Round Table" *see* "Round Table"
Writer's Schedule A, 72, 111
Writing, time for, 31

Y

"Your Cheatin' Heart," 6

www.ingramcontent.com/pod-product-compliance
Lightning Source LLC
LaVergne TN
LVHW031629070426
835507LV00024B/3407